The
Women's Stage Monologues
of 1997

Other books by Jocelyn A. Beard

100 Men's Stage Monologues from the 1980s

100 Women's Stage Monologues from the 1980s

The Best Men's/Women's Stage Monologues of 1990

The Best Men's/Women's Stage Monologues of 1991

The Best Men's/Women's Stage Monologues of 1992

The Best Men's/Women's Stage Monologues of 1993

The Best Men's/Women's Stage Monologues of 1994

The Best Men's/Women's Stage Monologues of 1995

The Best Men's/Women's Stage Monologues of 1996

The Best Stage Scenes for Men from the 1980s

The Best Stage Scenes for Women from the 1980s

The Best Stage Scenes of 1992

The Best Stage Scenes of 1993

The Best Stage Scenes of 1994

The Best Stage Scenes of 1995

The Best Stage Scenes of 1996

The Best Stage Scenes of 1997

Monologues from Classic Plays 468 B.C. to 1960 A.D.

Scenes from Classic Plays 468 B.C. to 1970 A.D.

100 Great Monologues from the Renaissance Theatre

100 Great Monologues from the Neo-Classical Theatre

100 Great Monologues from the 19th C. Romantic & Realistic Theatre

Smith and Kraus *Books For Actors*
THE MONOLOGUE SERIES
The Best Men's / Women's Stage Monologues of 1997
The Best Men's / Women's Stage Monologues of 1996
The Best Men's / Women's Stage Monologues of 1995
The Best Men's / Women's Stage Monologues of 1994
The Best Men's / Women's Stage Monologues of 1993
The Best Men's / Women's Stage Monologues of 1992
The Best Men's / Women's Stage Monologues of 1991
The Best Men's / Women's Stage Monologues of 1990
One Hundred Men's / Women's Stage Monologues from the 1980's
2 Minutes and Under: Character Monologues for Actors
Street Talk: Character Monologues for Actors
Uptown: Character Monologues for Actors
Ice Babies in Oz: Character Monologues for Actors
Monologues from Contemporary Literature: Volume I
Monologues from Classic Plays
100 Great Monologues from the Renaissance Theatre
100 Great Monologues from the Neo-Classical Theatre
100 Great Monologues from the 19th C. Romantic and Realistic Theatres
A Brave and Violent Theatre: 20th C. Irish Monologues, Scenes & Hist. Context
Kiss and Tell: Restoration Monologues, Scenes and Historical Context
The Great Monologues from the Humana Festival
The Great Monologues from the EST Marathon
The Great Monologues from the Women's Project
The Great Monologues from the Mark Taper Forum
YOUNG ACTOR SERIES
Great Scenes and Monologues for Children
Great Monologues for Young Actors
Multicultural Monologues for Young Actors
SCENE STUDY SERIES
Scenes From Classic Plays 468 B.C. to 1960 A.D.
The Best Stage Scenes of 1997
The Best Stage Scenes of 1996
The Best Stage Scenes of 1995
The Best Stage Scenes of 1994
The Best Stage Scenes of 1993
The Best Stage Scenes of 1992
The Best Stage Scenes for Men / Women from the 1980's

If you require pre-publication information about upcoming Smith and Kraus books, you may receive our semi-annual catalogue, free of charge, by sending your name and address to *Smith and Kraus Catalogue, 4 Lower Mill Road, North Stratford, NH 03590. Or call us at (800) 895-4331, fax (603) 922-3348.*

The Best
Women's Stage Monologues
of 1997

edited by Jocelyn A. Beard

The Monologue Audition Series

SK
A Smith and Kraus Book

Published by Smith and Kraus, Inc.
One Main Street, Lyme, NH 03768

First Edition: August 1998
10 9 8 7 6 5 4 3 2

The Monologue Audition Series ISSN 1067-134X

NOTE: These monologues are intended to be used for audition and class study; permission is not required to use the material for those purposes. However, if there is a paid performance of any of the monologues included in this book, please refer to the permissions acknowledgment pages to locate the source who can grant permission for public performance.

Contents

Preface

It hardly seems possible that another theatrical season has passed by, yet here I am, finishing up yet another volume of stage monologues for women while getting started on a brand new one. (I need a vacation, someone tell Marisa and Eric!)

1997 saw many interesting things happen on stage. Of particular note was a return to the classics via slick contemporary adaptations. *Epic Poetry, Polaroid Stories, Icarus* and *Noah's Archives* all offer fresh new looks at familiar stories and characters, offering the actress the opportunity to dig deeply into her bag of tricks for the solid archetypal material she stowed there before heaping all the complexities of contemporary story-telling on top. These plays find the woman as the wandering adventurer, side by side with (rather than opposed to) man. The roles in these plays are very interesting indeed for actresses bored with kitchen-sink whiners from "poor poor pitiful me" dramas and are well worth a look-see.

While reading scripts for this book I encountered a number of monologues belonging to characters that are just plain weird…that's a good weird, not a bad weird, mind you. For those of you looking for something off the beaten track, check out the monologues from *Big Bang, Easter, L'Eboueur Sleeps Tonight, Scared Of Demons* and *Svetlana's New Flame*. The characters in these plays are fascinating; some funny some not, but all compelling and ultimately cool. These gals will get a director's attention—gar-run-teed.

I discovered nice, solid dramatic monologues in *A Garden Of Women, Jackie: An American Life, The Joy Luck Club, Whiteout, Molly's Delicious, Four Queens—No Trump* and *Scotland Road.*

(For those of you who don't already know, *Scotland Road* is a ghostly tale of love and loss on board a certain famous luxury liner whose name began with a "T.")

Slightly more comedic offerings were found in *Gunshy, Lions, Tigers And Bears, Marcus Is Walking, Tea Time,* and *Drawing Down Clio.*

Younger actresses (age 20 and under) should check out *Epic Poetry, Molly's Delicious, The Northern Lights, Polaroid Stories, Soda Fountain* and *Sticky And Shary.*

My personal favorite from this collection came to me from across the sea via the magic of the world wide web. *Twockers, Knockers And Elsie Smith* by Jean Stevens is a gem of a one woman show for an actress over fifty. Since there aren't many incredible roles (let alone entire plays) written for women of mature years, I thought it worth mentioning.

Remember: if you find something you like…READ THE PLAY!

This book is dedicated to all the Elsie Smiths of the world, including my own incredible mom, Marilyn "Elsie Smith" Cole Greene. Long may you rock!

Spring 1998
The Brickhouse
Patterson, NY

Bad Grrrls

Linda Eisenstein

Scene: here and now

Serio-Comic
Meg: (20–30) a young woman momentarily dazzled by a glimpse of life's Big Picture

> *Here, impatient Meg reveals the brief yet profound epiphany she experienced while waiting for a friend in the rain.*

MEG: So there I am after the show, cooling my heels in the Playhouse Square* lobby
(Note: insert the name of your big-buck commercial theatre here: the one that would present the touring production of "Cats".)
MEG: for what seems like hours, because as usual Dana was late AGAIN! And I'm waiting, and waiting, and waiting for the damn car to show up, and there's no sight of Dana, of course, and I've called the apartment twice and gotten the answering machine twice, and I figure she's probably in some book store browsing around without a care in the world, or having a second cup of Cafe Latté blabbing away with somebody, losing track of time while I'm just standing here looking stupid.

And so I think about maybe getting a cab, and I look in my wallet and discover I don't have enough money for one, and I'm getting more and more steamed, and more and more freaked out, until I can't even pay attention to the book I brought for this very purpose, because all I do is look up every ten seconds wishing the goddamn car and goddamn Dana would GET here, already, and soon all I'm doing is pacing up and down.

Until now it finally IS a whole hour that I've been waiting, and they actually make me switch lobbies, and they're starting to run the big industrial-sized vacuum cleaner and there's nobody there but me and the security guard and he wants to go home. And the frustration is starting to turn into panic and I'm muttering to myself, on the verge of hysteria, swearing I'm going to kill Dana the moment the car pulls up, that is, if she's not already dead from a traffic accident...

And THEN it starts to rain. And I totally lose it, man, I'm standing there staring out the glass doors, wracking sobs are pouring out of me, I'm actually sobbing with rage and loss and the sense of abandonment, feeling like a total fucking orphan of the storm, okay? And you know what happens then?

A homeless guy walks by. *(Pause.)* Outside. In the rain. A homeless guy walks by. And boom, two words light up my mind like a sudden flash of lightning, and I hear a voice. And it says: "Ungrateful girl."

It's my grandmother's voice. Not an angry voice, I don't ever remember her being angry. She'd just get this tone of regret, shaking her head, like you just didn't understand something. *(A sigh.)* "Ungrateful girl." And it's like a sword in my heart.

You know, I don't mean to be ungrateful. Really. I don't. It's not the way I was raised. "Be grateful for small favors." Grandma used to say stuff like that all the time. When you'd complain about some injury, like a teacher was nasty, or your feet hurt, she'd shrug and say "some people don't have any legs." Or, "people are starving in Armenia," she'd say, as she filled your plate with food you didn't want.

Well, they're starving in Armenia again, Grandma. And in Bosnia, and Chechnya, and a bunch of other places I can barely pronounce, but they all sound like places my grandmother could have been from. I could be from there. I could be living in one of those places now, starving and ducking bombs, if my grandmother hadn't gotten the hell out. Gotten out when she was still an ungrateful girl herself. A servant girl, who refused to listen to some priest's sermon about her duty. A hungry servant girl, who stole meat from her master's dog.

I figure that must be why we're all so ungrateful, so restless here. America is bubbling over with the genepool of the people who wouldn't sit still. We're all the children and grandchildren and great grandchildren of the ones who refused to sit and take whatever was dished out. So we're all congenitally ungrateful, you and I. We sit in our houses surrounded by riches and privilege and every convenience and advantage, bitching and moaning our heads off. Ungrateful, ungrateful.

Some places we would be illegal. Things I do, things I take for granted every day, could get me thrown in jail somewhere else. Tortured. Even killed. Did you see the pictures of those Iranian women, the ones who wouldn't wear the veil? With the black sacks over their heads, right before the trapdoor sank under their feet? That could be me. Or you. And I'm still fucking ungrateful, and so are you, I can see it in your eyes.

And why not? I don't think I should have to rejoice just because I'm not locked up. Why shouldn't freedom be the norm? Am I supposed to feel good because I only get dirty looks instead of a boot in the back or a truncheon to the head? Not hardly. Not hardly.

But it got to me, man. When I was standing there, watching that guy walk by in the rain. And I thought, maybe this life—this life in which I feel like I'm suffering so much, this life where I cry and cry—this one's the reward. It's time off for good behavior, man. Maybe in the last bunch of lives, they *really* got me— burned me as a witch, or shot me and left me in a ditch with the other corpses, or left me starving in some rathole for the jailers to rape. This life? This one's the reward. The one where they don't gouge my eyes out. The one where all I get is the occasional sneer, and a stack of unpaid bills, and a lover that leaves me standing alone in the lobby for an hour after some fluffy Broadway touring show, where the ticket cost more than some-body's Third World paycheck.

Oh, Jesus. I'm supposed to be standing here feeling grateful. Grateful for only being marginalized and misunderstood and ignored now and then. Hey, that's a piece of cake, babe. That's ice cream and butterflies and a walk in the park.

And then this car finally pulls up in the rain, fenders rattling—and there's Dana, with that look, you know, that guilty "I really fucked up, go ahead and walk on my face with your hob-nailed boots" hunched-over LOOK—and all I could think of was—Oh, babe. Oh, babe. We don't know how lucky we are.

Big Bang

Ellen Reif

Scene: here and now

Serio-Comic
Mabel: (11) a young victim

Here, an eleven year-old girl waits in the hall outside speech class and confides a troubling experience (in a roundabout way) to a friend.

MABEL: *(To herself.)* Abra Cadabra peanut butter and jelly sandwiches abra cadabra peanut butter and jelly sandwiches abra cadabra peanut butter and jelly sandwiches abra cadabra peanut butter and jelly sandwiches abra cadabra peanut butter and jelly sandwiches abra cadabra peanut butter and *(To classmate.)* I didn't mean to steal his hair. It was an accident. I wasn't even thinking about it. I just did it. Fair trade. I didn't even know at first. Can you believe it? I didn't even know, I'm so dumb. Sometimes. See my barrettes my barrettes Lucy gave me didn't fly out of my hair when we hit that car. I thought when I sat up they wouldn't be there. I was worried they flew right out. Right out the window. But they didn't they were right here, right here when I sat up. They didn't slide, not an inch, not a half an inch not a centimeter not one-sixteenth of a centimeter. Nothing. They were in the exact same place I put them. Here. Here. It wouldn't have happened on Monday because on Monday I had thin stringy hair but now I have thick luxorious hair. Look, look, it's thicker and longer. On Monday I did the standing broadjump and I wore my barrettes for good luck but I didn't win. I jumped and when I landed they flew out of my hair and they landed too. Right in front of me. They beat me and they beat Susan Jacobs by a half an inch but they were disqualified because they don't count. Because they're barrettes. But it would have been funny anyways if it had happened. But it didn't. I would've laughed.

Abra Cadabra peanut butter and jelly sandwiches abra cadabra peanut butter and jelly sandwiches abra cadabra peanut

I've lost a red bead. I gave Lucy a green yellow and orange bead to wear in her barrettes and Lucy gave me a blue red and white bead to wear in mine. She wanted to give me a blue white and white bead to wear. But no! That's not fair. That's not a fair trade. So she gave me a red one and I lost it.

Abra cadabra peanut butter and jelly sandwiches abra cadabra peanut butter and jelly sandwiches

He knows he knows that I stole his hair I know he does he's such a stupid...stupid...STUPID! That's why I'm here today on Wednesday I only have speech class on Mondays and Fridays never on Wednesdays that's why he called me here and that's why he's making me wait so long in this hallway because...he's scared of me. I just want a fair trade

A FAIR TRADE

Abra cadabra peanut butter and jelly sandwiches

That was on Sesame Street when he was pinching me tickling me on top of me inside of me

On his desk

Abra Cadabra

There's a kiddie class next door kindergarteners and they were watching Sesame Street very berry loud that's all I could hear and my hand was in his hair when...cadabra...

He stole from me

I think it was Elmo

It had to be Elmo because Elmo is wonderful

And that's all I could hear those words those magic words Elmo whispered my friend Elmo which I whispered to myself when my hand was in his hair and he was...

(Pause.) I stole from him

Me

Me. I took it.

Peanut butter and jelly sandwiches

I stole his hair and now it's mine. And I'm not giving it back. Ever. And the bald spot he has is going to grow and grow he'll lose everything his hair and it'll grow and grow onto his face he'll lose his eyes ears nose mouth chin legs. He'll look like Mr. PotatoHead with no accessories, nothing. And I'll have it all. All of it.
Abra Cadabra Peanut Butter and Jelly Sandwiches
Fair Trade

Big Bang
Ellen Reif

Scene: here and now

Serio-Comic
Susie: (20s) a young woman who has just hit her boyfriend with his car

> *Here, a remorseful Susie pleads for her boyfriend's life in the ER.*

SUSIE: *(To her boyfriend.)* I'm sorry, oh my God I'm sorry. You're gonna pull through you gotta pull through cause I need you to live because I need you. To love me. Because no one loves me like you love me. There are no mistakes with you that's why I can be honest. I've always been dishonest because nobody loved me, everybody hated me, but you gave me unconditional love and there's nothing like it. *(Addressing a nurse.)* Please please you've got to save him so he can love me. I ran over him with his car but I'm sorry I'm truly sorry. *(To boyfriend.)* Honey of course I'm sorry. I wouldn't say I'm sorry if I didn't mean it. I mean maybe before, before when I didn't trust you I might have lied. Like when I gave you gonorrhea and I didn't tell you and then I acted like you gave it to me. God, I was so childish I'm so sorry. Now I would've said "Look ya dumbass, yes of course I gave you gonorrhea, where else would you have gotten it from, your dirty underwear? You got it, deal with it." Probably catching me and your father in the kitchen was the best thing for me. For the first minute you know what I was thinking? "Holy shit, that's it, it's over it's over it's over." And then you, you were so cute, you didn't say a word, you just stopped and kind of did this cute little freeze, took five dramatic steps backwards, closed the door and you let us finish. And the second I heard you lock that door that very second, that was the second I fell in love with you. *(To Nurse.)* You've got to save this man *(To boyfriend.)* And I've only been in love with you. Only you. Any of my past boyfriends, if I had gotten drunk and burned their church down, they would have never stood by me like you did. But you were intelligent enough to step back from the situation and say "Okay, I bought her five shots of tequila knowing she can only handle four, I gave her matches when I knew she didn't smoke and I mentioned that being a Methodist was beginning to turn me off from God." Okay. I hit that deer. That was a bad decision I was curious. But you didn't have to call me an asshole. I could lie, you know, I could lie to you, I could say that my foot got tired and accidentally hit the gas pedal. But that's not true. I'm telling you the truth because I respect you. I slammed that pedal. You know why? Because you're right. I am an asshole. I'd rather be candy but that's why you love me. I want to be with you the rest of my life! Live!

By the Sea, By the Sea, By the Beautiful Sea: "Day"

Lanford Wilson

Scene: a beach during the week of the Perseid Meteor Showers

Serio-Comic
Bill: (30s) a confused, chemically-dependent American aristocrat

*When she visits her lover at the beach where he works, Bill
(who has recently been released from rehab) reveals her fear
and loathing of the ocean.*

BILL: *(She looks at the ocean.)* I don't like it. I don't like to go to
the beach. The ocean's—look at it. It's too profound. It's too—
bigger than I am. And stronger, and deeper, it knows things. I
don't think it's thoughtless. I think it's evil. You see the white caps
and a fizzy surf or something, when you get your boat in the
water, taking people out for trips, sail boats and sunsets. I just
see—all the people who've gone down to their death; sailors,
Pearl Harbor, the Lusitania, fucking Titanic. I look out like, it's just
saying to me: "Bill, I don't give a fuck about you! You could jump
off the boat, I'd take you down, I'd never think a thing about it.
I'd still make the same flop against the side of the boat, the same
surf sound. You'll never even have the satisfaction to catch me
gloating." Only that fucker is always gloating. You know those
cable-knit sweaters? Fishermen's sweaters? Got those braids
down the front? Those got started in Ireland cause every mother
knitted a different pattern so when her men folk drowned, got
fished up all rotten, she could recognize his sweater and identify
him. I'd never wear one of those; like wearing a body bag. The
ocean doesn't take responsibility for its actions, and that sucks.
Before you get all romantic about it, the ocean is just this hired
hit man. Only hit woman. The ocean is a "she." Of course. "She's

10

rough today." Boy…! You *know men* don't trust it. Anything they don't understand, scares the shit out of them, they call it "She." Evil piece of— *(Yelling out.) I'm on to you, bitch! (And for no good reason she hits at Ace, slapping his shoulders.)*

The Dark Parent

Victor Bravo

Scene: here and now

Dramatic
Carol: (40s) a woman whose daughter has disappeared

> *Weeks after Anna has disappeared without a trace, Carol has*
> *slowly returned to her life where she is haunted by dark*
> *dreams of her daughter's most likely demise.*

CAROL: It's been six weeks since I last talked to my daughter. She's still the foremost part of my life, and for that, she'll forever hold power over me. I teach children piano and drama everyday and often see her face in one of their faces, or hear her voice in one of their voices. The visions of the three strangers have gone away. I refute that vision. Maybe I'm naive, but I refuse to accept the end of her. I refuse to accept the arbitrariness of a violent world. So strongly do I feel her alive, that the telephone, an otherwise inanimate object that I've always hated, has become the center of my world at home. No matter what I'm doing, it always seems to draw my attention. I wait for it to ring. Periods between rings are transitional, unreal times. And when the person on the other end is not her, I chat amiably, set the receiver down, and wait for it to ring again. In very weak moments I pray to the phone. The phone has become my god. *(Pause.)* No, the three strangers have leaped into my husband's consciousness. He would have it no other way. He stayed in New Orleans another week after I returned to Texas. He called Detective Sorensen everyday to see if anyone had made an attempt to claim the car. No one had. He made the rounds of clubs and restaurants, believing intensely with each new morning that this was going to be the day he found her. That was his way of exhausting all possibilities. He doesn't understand the possibilities are endless. He wants to believe she's alive, but darkness has always won with him. So, he's returning to the French Quarter next weekend to ask people his heartfelt questions and show them her picture. *(Pause.)* I can't do that. Now, I do what he used to. I stare out the window into the driveway at three in the morning, waiting for her to pull up. I stare dreamily, until her car, blurry, creeps alongside the front garden, and her face, tired but glorious, catches the porchlight as she climbs out and walks toward the house.

> *(A pool of light captures a beaming Anna. She turns to Carol.)*

CAROL: And I don't think it's silly at all.

Dialogue of Self and Soul

Jo J. Adamson

Scene: a psychiatrist's office

Dramatic
Anne: (30s) a woman coming to grips with her tragic childhood

> *Here, Anne reveals a childhood filled with horror and abuse during a particularly intense therapy session.*

ANNE: When I was five years old my father locked me and my pregnant mother in the dining room of our house and didn't let us out for over a year. *(Anne's voice breaks. She loses control.)* Why don't you have a couch! Aren't all practicing psychiatrists suppose to have a couch. What kind of therapist are you?

[SIMMS: I prefer a frontal confrontation.]

ANNE: *(Mock-seductive.)* doctor, I didn't know you cared.

[SIMMS: Go on Anne.]

(Anne gets up.)

ANNE: *It hurts.*

[SIMMS: A year is a long time to spend in a room. What did you do?]

ANNE: We camped there my mother and I. Busied ourselves with books and magazines and when we tired of that we listened to the serials on the radio. We slept a lot. I don't remember relieving myself, or what I ate. I didn't know whether it were summer or winter. I learned not to ask questions. I had a cardboard box of cigarette wrappers. I wadded these up in a silver ball. When we finally got out it was the size of a basketball. When the pains came mama left me for awhile to have the baby. I hardly knew she was gone. Sometimes I told time by the radio programs. "The Buster Brown Gang" was my favorite. I knew it was between 11:30 and 12:00 when that came on. I loved all the heroes. "Baba," an Arabian boy with a horse. "Ghangi," a Hindu lad with an elephant named Teelah. "Little Fox" an American Indian boy, and "Kulah" who had Jug-Genie. *(Anne cannot look at Simms. She's back in the past.)* I was listening to Jug-Genie when Mama sneaked the baby in. She showed me all the cute baby clothes and let me hold her. I was afraid to breathe because I was eating saltine crackers and I thought my breath would form saline crystals on her delicate skin.

Mama told me that daddy was sick. He was suffering from nerve gas exposure. Exposure to war was what he suffered from. That was enough to make anyone mad. The doctor had told Mama that he would be all right with a whole lot of tender loving care. Mama said he had nightmares before she went into the dining room with me. He used to wake up at night and try to choke her. She had to wear a scarf around her neck for two weeks. She told the neighbors she had a neck cold. I was to be very quiet when anyone came to the house. It would embarrass Daddy, Mama said, to have people learn that he had to hide his wife and daughters. I said it didn't make any difference because I'd disappeared for him about six months ago. Faded like the grin off the Cheshire Cat. When the baby cried, Mama would hold her against her breast and give her milk. I thought she was suffocating the baby. But she said a baby couldn't suffocate in her mother's skin. I wasn't sure. She had to put the nipple in her mouth or the baby would starve. "Imagine Annie," Mama said, "being so dependent." I was not to make a sound when someone came to check on Daddy. Especially when Aunt Alice came. She didn't get along with Frederick. When she asked where we were, Daddy said we had gone to the ocean and laughed as if he had something caught in his throat.

Drawing Down Clio

Doug Baldwin

Scene: an ad agency in Portland, Oregon

Serio-Comic
Teddie: (40s) president of an ad agency, recently widowed

> *Teddie has returned to the office following a lengthy bereavement. Here, she describes a perfectly miserable Christmas.*

TEDDIE: I have just had the worst Christmas of my life. It was torture. Sheer torture. I mean…He's dead, Leo's *been* dead, for weeks, but I just haven't been able to get through the mourning part of it. So, this holiday season, instead of red and green, everything was black. Black black black. Did you know you can actually get black ornaments for your tree? Well, you can. They sell them at the funeral home. Boy, they suck those Christmas lights right out of their sockets. *(Makes a sucking noise.)* Our tree looked like a six-foot black hole. With tinsel. To cheer me up, everybody bought me blouses. *(Models her blouse.)* Ta-da! Seven blouses, size twelve—all black. All wrapped in shiny black paper. It's comforting, in a way: despite being in deep bereavement, I have remained color-coordinated. So, there I am Christmas morning, my first in I-don't-know-how-many years without Leo— slightly sauced, dressed like Darth Vader, lurching around the house, blubbering all over the place. My poor kids kept steering me away from the tree. I think they were afraid I'd be sucked into that black hole. It was really the most miserable holiday you can imagine. Bing Crosby's worst nightmare—a black Christmas. I mean, Santa and the Grim Reaper: what a team.

Easter

William Scheffer

Scene: the rural Mid-West

Dramatic
Wilma: (20-30) a woman driven over the edge of reason by the
death of her child

> *Wilma and her husband, Matthew, have been on the run
> since the death of their baby. Wilma has burned down a
> dozen or more churches in a tragic effort to express her feel-
> ings of guilt and rage. Here, she muses about her growing
> disassociation from the world.*

WILMA: *(Calmly.)* You know Matty, I haven't read a newspaper
since we came out here. I don't think I should read newspapers.
I don't like the way they put things. They set me to worrying too
much about the world. About the future of the world. About the
children of the future.

[MATTHEW: Uh-huh.]

WILMA: I think it was all those reports about the ozone layer and
the green house effect. And that big earthquake in California.
That really shook me up. And when we were in Wichita all I'd
have to do is look out the window, and it was just so…dry outside. You know, it just doesn't rain like it used to back in Taloga,
and I kept thinking about the children of the future surrounded
by all that…dryness, and it would get me…agitated.

[MATTHEW: That s good.]

WILMA: There's just so much dust everywhere. I think I'm gonna
take up gardening. Gonna get me some nice Burpee seed cata-
logues and just forget about the six o'clock news. God they'd
make you think there was nothing but unpleasant things going
on in the world. Miracle Whip?

[MATTHEW: Yeah sure.]

(Wilma's sandwich making has become ritualistic. She is piling cold-cuts and Wonderbread on top of one another, creating huge sandwich sculptures.)

WILMA: *(Calm and centered.)* Its just that everything is changing. I'm changing, the whole world is changing. Sometimes when bad things happen, when things burn down, it's to make way for something new to be born. When I let those news stories get to me like that, I just didn't understand the information! You see, mudslides, wildfires, earthquakes, they aren't such bad things. God, California! When I imagine California I just have to hold my breath, I have this tremendous identification with California.

(Wilma has stopped making sandwiches. She holds her belly. She is listening to something. Matthew has taken notice.)

[MATTHEW: You O.K.?]

WILMA: It's like there's an earthquake inside of me. Like I'm the San Andreas Fault. My God, I'm becoming enormous.

[MATTHEW: Wilma?]

WILMA: Oh I can't help it. The Virgin did speak to me. She said I was chosen.

[MATTHEW: No. It was just a figment.]

WILMA: Matthew. I feel the rumblings of things to come.

[MATTHEW: Oh God no. *(He moves to hug her.)*]

WILMA: *(A touch of St. Joan.)* No! You don't need to touch me! You just need to listen. I've been informed. *(Pause.)* When Easter comes—the stars will speak to me. God is coming.

[Matthew races from the cabin.]

WILMA: And I'm not going crazy.

Epic Poetry

James Bosley

Scene: a mythical time in the New York tri-state area, specifically the underworld

Dramatic
Lief: (15) a young woman in search of her father

> *Lief has left Penelope, her mother, to go in search of her missing father, Ulysses. When she falls into a river, she drowns and dies. Here, Lief wakes up dead in Pluto's underworld.*

LIEF: Oh God, I'm dead. I'm dead. I'm really dead. This is not what I had in mind. Adventure, yeah. Danger, of course. But death? How stupid I am! I didn't know I could actually die! I mean I knew but I never realized—Mamma! I'm sorry for being so stupid mamma. You'll be so upset. And I'm sorry for not liking Albert. He's okay I guess. Please make this a dream. Please make this a dream. Daddy, I died looking for you. I hope you'll know that. Hope? There is no hope for me. Never see the Taj Majal. Never learn to rollerblade. Never read the Argonautica. Never see my father. Never have a family of my own. Never even have sex. Damn. I was looking forward to that.

F.O.B. To U-Haul: New York Lessons

Steven Tanenbaum

Scene: NYC

Serio-Comic
Woman: (30s) a New Yorker

> *Here, a denizen of the Big Apple ruminates on the city's more esoteric qualities.*

WOMAN: New York City is often referred to as a Mecca: A Mecca of finance; a Mecca of culture and even a Mecca of decadence. But it is seldom referred to as a Mecca in the oldest sense of the word: a holy city. But I have witnessed many examples of New York's spiritual character. I think I even had a religious epiphany watching some elderly Chinese practice Tai Chi at four in the morning in Tompkins Square Park during a blizzard—but I don't want to fast forward to that part yet. I want to focus on a specific type of spiritual dispensation that is peculiar to this city. You see, on occasion, if you're really fortunate, you can be a witness to the unique brand of Karma that New York renders. The luck depends, of course, on which end of the Karmic intercourse you're on. Trust me, it's best not to be on the bottom when New York City decides to fuck you. Don't scoff: this is no new age psycho babble. If you think about it for a second, you'll realize that you too have met the appointed messengers of New York's Karmic justice. They're all around us, lurking in the shadows, just waiting for you to turn out the light; so they can come out of hiding and put the fear of god in your heart. Next time you practice the profane art of double dealing; just wait 'til you get home, the agents of New York Karma will be lying in wait for you. When you least expect it, and you're at your most vulnerable, like at two

AM, when you've gotten out of bed to pee; don't flick the switch on in the bathroom, because without a doubt, the biggest mother-fucking cockroach—I'm talking strictly waterbug variety—will be camping out on your toilet seat, mocking your bare-footed predicament...You aren't officially a New Yorker until you've scraped cockroach custard off the bottom of your bare foot—Check it out: everytime you fuck someone over in this city, a mutant waterbug comes-a-knocking. I don't care if you live in a penthouse or the projects—it's true.

Forget-Me-Not

Richard Lay

Scene: an apartment in NYC

Serio-Comic
Rosie: (44) an artist

> *After an evening of drinking, Rosie has returned to her apart-
> ment with three men in tow. Here, she explains her motives.*

ROSIE: NO. *(To audience.)* Why do I do it? Why am I attracted to
excess? I paint, I paint because I can't help it. I paint every day
from when the sun blesses my drunken face. And then I drink
while I paint. Hunger pangs are usually preludes to naps, which I
take—often. It seems to me that I only eat on Fridays…a peculiar
life-style you might think. I smoke like a trooper and sometimes
dip chips into red or green—I prefer the green—salsa. I tire of
them quickly and then smoke. Oh yes, I smoke a lot. Let the nico-
tine line my lungs and give me that friendly morning cough. I
used to have a boy friend in Alaska and I used to have an intel-
lectual husband. What good did they do me? I can understand
the torture I must have given them…but I am me. I can't change.
Won't change. Both of them said to me that one day I would be
on the streets asking for change. I don't think so…Van Gogh and
Monet and Manet were all desperate people. I do not copy them.
I copy nobody. My technique is unique *(Theatrical tear.)* …please
let me be UNIQUE…And now I am here in my small New York
apartment with three men…a black footballer, a sweet
Colombian drug dealer and a silent Irishman who looks as if he
could be good in bed—whatever that means…I used to know,
once in a blue moon. *(Feeling sorry for herself.)* I don't know
what I really need. Probably death…an early exit on a summer's
day and an elegant funeral on a shoe-string—attended by the
ones who admire me most. They will weep. There she goes,

Rosie, there will never be another one like her they will think through their tears…rose petals on my casket…Californian Chardonay and cheese at my wake and the reading of telegrams from all the people who couldn't be there. Friends will wail and collapse over my coffin—and that bastard Jude will play a lament on his Strad. He will play it badly on purpose, just for me. As for now…my looks flirt with danger. In truth, I suppose I mean age. No wrinkles yet. Just worries. I get phone calls about my promiscuity from old boy friends who have pictures of me on their walls…The way I saw it and lived it was very simple—I would go into a room and say to any new good friend…I will sleep with him and him and him. I got to the point where I didn't know who'd I'd slept with the night before…when I woke up they were never there. I used to worry when they didn't call back…So now I'm forty-four and I couldn't care a damn who listens…doesn't listen. *(Calmly.)* I am just Rosie. I will paint my paintings and talk to as many men as I want and when I want. The consequences are insignificant because I really don't care.

Four Queens—No Trump

Ted Lange

Scene: a card game

Serio-Comic
Deola: (30s) a hard-working African American business woman who can also predict the future

> *Deola is host to a weekly game of bid whist at which she and her friends meet to play cards and share their lives. On this particular evening, she is cooking chitlins, much to the olfactory consternation of her friends. Here, she gamely defends chitlins' place in American culinary history.*

DEOLA: I'll have you know chitlins are good for the soul.

[MAUDE: Okay, Deola, what kind of metaphor are you drawing now?]

DEOLA: I don't mean figuratively. I mean literally.

[JOCENIA: You're saying that chitlins are literally good for your soul?]

DEOLA: Yep!

[MAUDE: How would my soul know?]

DEOLA: It can smell them too. The odor of chitlins can reach deep down into your soul.

[JOCENIA: Amen to that, Sister.]

[MAUDE: Dee, oh please!]

DEOLA: The long time survival of the chiterling as a food group has fed a nation of black folk. Think back to that magic moment when the master had given us only table scraps and some proud black woman said as she walked through the kitchen, "I rather eat the garbage end of a pig, than endure the humiliation of fighting for massa's left-overs." Being a black woman of some ingenuity, imagination, and substance, plus a damn good cook, she labored over the entrails of some unfortunate swine.

[JOCENIA: Preach, Sister!]

DEOLA: Having secured the basic element to her southern cuisine, namely a whole lot of pig guts, she took her booty back to the kitchen.

[JOCENIA: And she took her black booty back to the kitchen, too.]

DEOLA: Precisely. There amongst the solitude of seven herbs and spices, she started to work her magic. She began to conjure and call on the gods of the four natural food groups: Come Pillsbury, Nabisco, and Ocean Spray, On Campbell's, Kellogg's, and Good Ol'Del Monte. Now boil away, boil away, boil away all. Into the pot she stirred her delights,

Pinching, and sifting, and measuring that.

Not hog mauls, but chitlins and greasy pig fat.

So when you've tasted the sting of defeat,

Remember a taste that's harder to beat,

It's not from a cow, horse, or a lamb,

It's the guts of a pig and all else be damned!

Four Queens—No Trump

Ted Lange

Scene: a card game

Dramatic
Edna: (30–40) An African American woman trying to restart her life after an unhappy marriage

> *Edna has begun dating a white man whose family, she has just discovered, comes from the same small town in Texas as does her own. It was in this small town that her grandmother was raped and beaten by a white lynch mob in 1922. Here, she remembers her grandmother's pain and her own efforts to bring the older woman some comfort.*

EDNA: There are so many things about Texas that I want to forget. My ex-husband. Growing up poor. Watching little white girls swim in segregated pools. But mostly it's the pain my Granny Laura suffered through. *(She stops, she is uncomfortable with the idea of continuing.)*

[DEOLA: Talk it out, It's good for you.]

EDNA: You know as a kid growing up in Texas, I had my chores that I had to do. My Mama didn't allow no shirking of any household duties. I'd cook the family breakfast. Wash and wax the kitchen floor on Saturdays. Make every bodies lunch for school. Iron clothes. But the hardest thing I ever had to do was tend to my Grannies crippled legs. *(She stops and looks at Deola.)*

[DEOLA: I'm listening.]

EDNA: I'd get up in the morning, and make her HILLS BROTHERS COFFEE. Black. Draw her bath water, then watch her have her saucer full of coffee. She'd pour her coffee in the saucer, blow it cool and sip it. Her gnarled hands barely able to hold the saucer. She hated drinking coffee from a cup. Dee, She had been beaten as a young woman, her once beautiful legs bent out of shape.

Deformed. Crippled from the beating. I'd add Epsom salt to the bath. Help her in the tub, and wash her. My mother and I would lift her out of the tub; Then later as I got older I could manage by myself. I'd dry her, then rub her legs with "Vaseline". Trying to massage her muscles, trying to bring life back to those legs. Trying to capture the past and rub away history. I used to try and massage a better and brighter future. I'd dig my hands into that "Vaseline," hold those crippled brown legs and I'd try and rub away her pain. With every step she took, she tried to walk away from her past. And now her past has caught up with me.

A Garden of Women

Ludmilla Bollow

Scene: the garden of the Wyndham Estate, 1920

Dramatic
Lorinda Wyndham: (30) a woman driven to dispair and madness by the death of her unborn child.

> *Once full of life, Lorinda has deteriorated in the years that have passed since she lost the baby she was carrying. She has decided to give the beautiful estate to an order of Catholic nuns and here comes to the garden a final time to bid her lost child farewell.*

LORINDA: *(Singing in despondent voice, meandering tones.)* "I come to the garden alone… *(Pause.)* While the dew is still on the roses… *(Pause.)* And the voice I hear—" *(Stops. Looks about in bewilderment, then goes to large rock that has been set in front of tree, kneeling before it.)* My child—My dear, dear child. I have not visited you for so many days, because—I could not visit you— And now I cannot take you with me… *(Walking away.)* I must leave—you and my lovely flowers… And never return… *(Sits on bench.)* Four months. One hundred and twenty days, I carried you inside me. We became so close. You were part of me, I was part of you. Only, you were so anxious to enter the world, forcing your way out, struggling to be born—long before you were ready. No way to stop you! *(Walking.)* Oh, they tried to save you at the hospital. Blood! Bleeding all over. Cutting you loose, tearing you from me. I wanted to follow—go wherever it was you went. None of my screaming brought you back. I—I couldn't just let them throw you out. So, I paid the nurse, to wrap you in the flowered blanket, the one I embroidered to take you home in. A tiny blob of flesh, that's all you were—but I could see—hands— feet— *(Stops at stone.)* So I buried you here, in my garden, under

this rock of granite, that still sparkles in the moonlight—
Reflecting the stars. Gathering my tears.

(First eight notes of "I Come to the Garden Alone" sounds in haunting single tones. Pause. Rises.)

LORINDA: When they told me after, I could have no more children—my mind became as torn apart as my body. And I had to go away—to be cured. But there is no cure—not for this everlasting pain...Richard tried—but what can men do about a pain that only women know. My only consolation, to come out here, talk to you, sing to you. And you always listened. Never left me... *(Walking about.)* But now, Richard has left me. Influenza. So horrible. I cannot live in this empty house anymore. Yet, I dare not sell, have strangers roll away your stone, dig up my garden... Oh, I want to leave you something, to keep you from crying, when you're all alone—without me. What? *(Looks about bewilderedly. Then wrings her hands. Suddenly, inspired.)* My grandmother Abigail's ring! You shall have this special ring of rubies and diamonds, that looks like a tiny radiant flower. *(On her knees, digging, laughing in giddy tones.)* I'll bury it now, here, in the earth—where you live. Then you'll always have a bright little flower with you—summer and winter. *(Half sings, half talks as she digs.)* "With rings on her fingers and bells on her toes—She shall have music, wherever she goes— *(Fading.)* An elephant to ride upon—" *(Sits.)* The melancholy is on me again. I need to rest... I came to tell you—I'm leaving Wyndham Place—to some very special ladies—Blessed women who will love and tend this garden. Who will pray for our souls. Sanctify this ground...

(The single notes of "I Come to the Garden" vibrates as Lorinda freezes. Pause, then suddenly paces about, screaming in a frenzy.)

LORINDA: No! It can't be! Where! What happened? I can't find my little angel anymore! Where did I hide the precious thing?... My head's all fuzzy—And my flowers, my beautiful lovely flowers—they were all just dancing a few moments ago, like bright shimmering jewels—now they're fading—Disappearing...Withering... *(Searching frantically.)* Where did everything go!! *(Whirls and stops before grotto.)* A spell has been cast over me. For years and years I've waited for it to be lifted. But there's no one left to kiss me anymore. No one…I can't move…My body has turned to stone…Help me…Somebody…Help me….

(Becomes stiff with arm outstretched, as "Garden" notes vibrate. Breaks into hysterical sobbing that continues even after lights have dimmed.)

Golden Elliot

Linda Stockham

Scene: here and now

Dramatic
Jolene: (42) a college professor

> *Surrounded by blue books, Jolene explodes with frustration at her students' lack of interest and initiative.*

JOLENE: *(Groaning.)* Oh, for *god* sake! It's such a simple essay question: "Discuss the treatment of nature in James Fenimore Cooper's *The Last of the Mohicans"!* *(She reads on for a few more lines, then slams the blue book down.)* Just simply coming to class would be more than enough to answer this essay. I spent two class sessions on how Cooper treats nature in the *Mohicans*. Where were you? Think, think, think. It's not the scene of action but the emotional atmosphere fashioned by the creatures in the story. That includes "non-human" creatures. Think about that horse screaming out its deepest agony and terror…Think of "the horrid shriek" in the wilderness! Think of what the cry of the innocent horse symbolizes. How many of you even read the book? *(She takes glass of iced tea, stands and walks away from the table and blue books.)* Every year they get worse. No one reads, no one goes to libraries, no one thinks…All for the superficial and the easiest way out…This is not what you died for Elliott. Heaven only knows if there was a reason at all for your death. Heaven? Ah! There is no heaven. Is there, Elliott? We know that there is no heaven, since there obviously is no *god*. There are only lies to control us and lead us into a world as shallowpated as a theme park. Maybe the problem is that no one sees any importance with a novel from out of the past…No empathy for a frightened horse left alone in a savage, unknown wilderness.

(Jolene goes back to the blue books. Mrs. Baylor enters.)
JOLENE: All college professors talk to themselves, Mom. You know why? It isn't because no one understands us or that we like to hear our own voices, although that might be true in many cases. No. It's because no one wants to listen to us. Our students least of all.

Gunshy

Richard Dresser

Scene: a condo in the Pacific Northwest

Serio-Comic
Evie: (40) a woman trying to reconstruct her life following a divorce

> *Evie has divorced Duncan and left him behind in New England. She now fancies herself in love with Carter, a fellow divorcee. Here, she describes the final days of her marriage with Duncan to Carter as they share a bottle of wine.*

EVIE: We were so lost we tried to celebrate our anniversary during the darkest days of our marriage. The whole dinner he only spoke to the waiter, ordering one drink after another. I couldn't just watch the marriage go up in flames, so I left. I'm waiting for a bus when suddenly there's a gun jammed in my ribs and a voice telling me to give it up, bitch. I screamed and fought him for my bag...it seemed as if my whole life was in that big dumb bag. And he got it. I ran after him, crying and screaming and when I finally stopped it was absolutely cold and silent up and down the street and I knew I was really all alone, I couldn't pretend there was anyone else. And I knew I'd better grab whatever I wanted out of this life because it was all going to end in the smallest, safest moments, buying groceries, walking the dog, watching my son play baseball. Jack had been a surprise, we never even talked about having a baby, and then, later, we always talked about having another. Standing on that desolate street, I knew the baby thing was just part of this dream I was living. I moved out so I could stop dreaming.
    [CARTER: Just like that.]
EVIE: All it took was a little urban crime.

Hazing the Monkey

Marcus A. Hennessy

Scene: Iowa

Serio-Comic
Sally: (20s) an unhappy wife

> *Sally has manipulated her husband's life in practically every regard as she here reveals in the heat of argument.*

SALLY: Two years ago, you begged me to marry you…
> [ROGER: Begged? I didn't beg you. But after you lost the baby, I knew I…]

SALLY: The point is, I'm the one who made the commitment to stick with you for the long haul. Because I believed in you. I had faith in your ability to provide as a man, even though at the time you were just some drunk singer in a dead-end band.
> [ROGER: But I thought you liked…]

SALLY: Look, we are in this thing together. TOGETHER! You know what I mean? This is a partnership. You know how much time and energy and love I've spent on this partnership? A shitload pardon my French. I got you off the bottle. I saved you from the perils of liquor. And I pulled you out of your hopeless dreams. That took one helluva lot of work pardon my French. And I helped you to get a job. A real job. You don't know what I went through with Fred and that pig of a sister-in-law Wanda Cooper to get you that first interview two years ago. She hates you. But I convinced her to give your application to the right people, and you got the job. Because of me. BECAUSE OF ME!
> [ROGER: Gee, sweetie, I didn't know…]

SALLY: There's alotta shit you don't know, Roger, pardon my French. So here we are, hun, living in a mobile home in a mobile home park in the middle of Iowa, and I hate it! I absolutely hate it!

[ROGER: But I thought you liked it here. You said that…]

SALLY: I said I liked it because you liked it. Maybe I fudged with the truth forgive me dear Lord. Think about it, Roger. A mobile home in a mobile home park in Iowa! You know what we are? Do you?

[ROGER: Well, I guess.]

SALLY: WE ARE A BULLSEYE FOR TORNADOES! That's what we are! Tornadoes will go out of their way to hit us here. We're easy pickin's. You never see a high-class neighborhood ravaged by a twister. Those houses are built solid. No, no, it's always a swath of destruction through some mobile home park where everything's built cheap and flimsy. I can't tell you how many stormy nights I just prayed and prayed and prayed that the twisters would stay clear of this place long enough for us to get out and into a solid home. And my friends, people I know from the church, they see me working at the store and they smile at me and I can just see those thought balloons over their heads like in the comic books…"Oh, look, there's pretty Sally Youngblood. She's such a nice girl and she has such a nice husband but they live in a mobile home. They'll be gone soon. Such a pity."

Icarus

Edwin Sanchez

Scene: a beach house

Serio-Comic
Altagracia: (30s) a woman whose face is noticeably deformed
and whose spirit is noticeably amazing

> *Altagracia has rescued her brother from the state hospital*
> *and is hiding with him in an empty beach house. Beau, a man*
> *claiming to know the owner of the house has arrived on the*
> *scene wearing a ski mask which he asserts hides a hideous*
> *face disfigured in a car crash. Here, Altagracia tells him about*
> *her high school prom in an effort to help him come to terms*
> *with his newfound ugliness.*

ALTAGRACIA: When I was a mere slip of a girl I went to my high
school prom. This is not gonna bring up any evil high school
memories, is it?

[BEAU: No, when I was a mere slip of a girl I skipped the prom.]
ALTAGRACIA: I hate you.

[BEAU: I hate you worse.]
ALTAGRACIA: I hate you best. *(They sip.)* I had no intention of like
going but my mother found out the theme was Mardi Gras and
that everyone had to wear a mask. She became like a woman
possessed. It mattered so much to her that I let myself be talked
into it. Let her spend money we didn't have on this beautiful red
velvet dress, let her make this gorgeous mask of feathers and
sequins. I even let her pay my cousin to take me. She took a
Polaroid of us and she and Primi waved us off. I thought my heart
was gonna pop out of my chest. There I was outside the gymna-
sium door, and on the other side, everyone who had ever made
my life hell for the past twelve years. The doors open, and all eyes
turn to face the fairy princess.

(She sips. Beau leans in almost in spite of himself.)

[BEAU: ...what happened?]

ALTAGRACIA: Not a single person recognized me. Not a soul. I was the mystery girl. If I could bottle any moment in my life that would be it. Then somebody figured out who I was. And they all looked away, like they were embarrassed for me. Like I had been caught trying to pull something off. But I fixed them. I took over the prom. I got in the middle of the dance floor with my arms spread out, taking up as much space as I could and I started spinning around. And while I was out there no one else dared to dance. They didn't have the guts to look me in the eye. It became my prom, all mine. *(She drains her beer.)* Sometimes, you just gotta make people feel uncomfortable. Make the golden people look away.

Icarus

Edwin Sanchez

Scene: a beach house

Serio-Comic
The Gloria: (40–60) an aging beauty

> *Here, a woman who is desperate to hold on to her looks describes going to a power party and encountering a new blonde.*

THE GLORIA: Excuse me.

[Mr. Ellis stares at her.]

THE GLORIA: Helloooo. I'm looking for my date. Um, how silly, I don't even know his name. He's a swimmer. He's very young, and very handsome and he's not doing me a favor, you know. I am not his mercy,...date. I wanted to tell him everything that had happened. He has some connections so I'm sure he'll be able to help me. Would you be a love and give him the shortest little message? Can you do that?

[Mr. Ellis nods, he places his suitcase on its side so the Gloria can sit on it.]

THE GLORIA: Ooooh. A gentleman. They are in scarce supply. This is how a goddess should be treated. Tell him, tell him that the party was fabulous. I was looking wonderful and I had the tiniest little pint of courage, just to steel my nerves and headed to this marvelous A list party. I was in shape, the lights were low and my eyes could still focus. I walked around, sort of knowing people but not really knowing anyone. And then this year's blonde walked in. Lovely girl! Full of shyness and living on promise. Her film has not been released yet but oh the inside buzz is very "promising." She is moist and new. I had been her. I looked at her and surprised myself by not hating her. Her glow. Did I glow like that? Everybody wants to make sure she catches them smiling at her.

Just in case she turns out to be the real thing. *(She smiles and winks.)* "Remember I smiled at you. Remember, you owe me." I need to warn her about the burden of possibility. With everyone surrounding her, how can she breathe? I take her a drink. My, this could be some photo op. Yesterday's Blonde and Tomorrow's Blonde. No one wants to give up their space next to her and who can blame them? Her heat was my heat and my heat was fabulous! I am by her side and she takes my hand and shakes it, giving me one of those glazed smiling faces. The one that says, "Thank you for worshipping, now move along." And I toss the drink in her face, followed by the glass, followed by my fist. I was thrown out. I was thrown away. How about that?…How about that? *(She rises.)* Tell him to come over whenever he gets in. But tell him, not the really beautiful one. He's cruel.

In Search of the Red River Dog

Sandra Perlman

Scene: the backyard of a trailer home in Deerfield, Ohio. August, 1978

Dramatic
Paulette: (late teens—early 20s) a woman who has just been raped by her husband

> *The death of their child has driven an irrevocable wedge between Paulette and her husband, Denny. On a hot night in August, Denny finally explodes with pent-up rage and sexual frustration, forever killing any chance the couple may have had to fix their marriage as she here describes.*

PAULETTE: It wasn't John Senior did this to me, Mama.

   [BERTIE: Thank you Jesus 'cause when he drinks Paulette he doesn't remember anything.]

PAULETTE: It was Denny.

   [BERTIE: What.]

PAULETTE: It was my husband did this to me and he was sober as a judge. But God help me, I did not scream out, even though I should have. I did not cry out even when I was in pain and it was wrong to keep so silent. I did not do anything, Mama, even when he did everything to me that is wrong between a man and a woman. It has to be wrong to do something like this, Oh God, it has to be wrong. But I just closed my eyes and did nothing. No! I did something, I pretended I was dead. Yes, I pretended I was dead and it was the same thing as being dead and then I didn't have to pretend anymore. It was the same. Because there was no love here last night, Mama. Not in this place. Not in him or me, not on this cold, hard ground where he took me down lower than the lowest place on God's earth. I was in hell, Mama. I was in hell last night in this place with that man and there was no love here last night, just this cold, hard metal of a man drilling in to a woman he didn't even know. Drillin' in to a woman who prayed she would die. Oh, Mama, I prayed I would die and there was no love in this place last night, just darkness and two strangers. Just me and a cold, fish-eyed man killing what was left of that young girl he once loved. Just me and somebody with no name, Mama, 'cause that man was not my husband and I was not his wife. No, no, there was no love in this place, and those people that were here last night are dead. Those people died last night Mama. Their souls and their vows are broken and they can never be together again.

[BERTIE: Oh God, forgive me, Paulette, I didn't know.]

PAULETTE: Funny, Mama, funny how when it was over he rolled right over and slept like a baby.

Jackie: An American Life

Gip Hoppe

Scene: JFK's funeral, 1963

Dramatic
Jackie: (30s) recently widowed in Texas

> *Here, Jackie Kennedy takes a moment to reflect upon her loss.*

JACKIE: People say that time heals all wounds. How much time? Years? Months? And what if some wounds are so deep they never heal? Isn't that just as much a part of life as anything else? The little things seem so huge to me now. Small moments...a Sunday morning, reading the paper, and having breakfast together, the children playing. Nothing important being discussed...just the feeling that you're with the person you love. A sense that everything is complete. Sometimes I'll wake in the morning, eager to tell him something and he's not there. *(Jackie is left alone on stage holding the flag.)* Jack told me that when he was a boy, sick so much of the time, he would lay in bed, and read the Knights Of The Round Table. That's how I think of him sometimes. A little boy...immersed in King Arthur...innocently building the foundations of his destiny. So, now he is a legend, he belongs to history...he belongs to the world. But I knew a man...I knew a husband and a father. And that belongs to me.

The Joy Luck Club

Susan Kim
From the Novel by Amy Tan

Scene: here and now

Dramatic
Ying-Ying St. Clair: (50–60) a woman divulging an old secret

> *Here, Ying-Ying tells her daughter the passionate and tragic story of her first husband.*

YING-YING: I married this man. It was long ago—twenty years before you even born. I was beautiful then, and became even more beautiful, all for him—

[LENA: But you weren't in love, were you? You couldn't have loved him, you loved Dad…]

YING-YING: Was not my choice. When someone joins your body, there is a part of your mind that swims to join him, even when is against your will.

[LENA: I don't think I want to hear this.]

YING-YING: Listen to me. It is because I had so much love then, that I came to have so much hate. My husband began to take many trips to the north. They became longer after he planted a baby in my womb. It was the north wind that blew my husband my way—so at night, I would open my bedroom window to blow his spirit back to me. But the wind was so strong, it blew my husband past my bedroom and out the door. I found he left me for others. An opera singer. Dancers and American ladies. Prostitutes. A girl cousin even younger than I was. I wanted to die. Instead, I took the baby from my womb before it could be born. You think I do not know what it means to not want a baby. When the nurses asked what they should do with the lifeless baby, I hurled a newspaper at them. I told them to wrap it like a fish and throw it in the lake. A tiger is gold and black because it has two ways.

The gold side leaps with its fierce heart. The black side stands still with cunning, seeing and not being seen, waiting patiently for things to come. After the bad man left me, I went to the country and I waited—and watched. After ten years, I went back to the city. That is where I met Clifford St. Clair.

[LENA: Dad.]

YING-YING: He was clean and pleasant. He bought me gifts: cheap things, worthless trinkets. He did not know how rich I was as a girl, how these gifts meant nothing to me.

[LENA: But he saved you! He took you away from that poor village you were living in and saved you!]

YING-YING: Maybe. But I made him wait for years like a dog in front of a butcher shop.

[LENA: Didn't you…didn't you love him?]

YING-YING: He rubbed my feet at night. He praised the food I cooked. How could I not love him? But it was the love of a ghost. Arms that encircled but did not touch.

[LENA: *(In tears, abruptly gets up to leave.)* I don't want to hear this. Why are you telling me this?]

(Ying grabs Lena by the wrist.)

YING-YING: You must hear what I have to say! I heard that my husband was dead. I thought this man had long ago drained everything from my heart. But now something strong and bitter flowed. So I let Saint marry me. I let the hunter come up to me and turn me into a tiger ghost. All this, and I did not care—for I had given up my *chi,* the spirit that caused me so much pain. And now Saint is a ghost. Now he and I can love equally.

[Lena is shaken by sobs.]

YING-YING: Now you know the pain that cut my spirit loose. And now I have told you, my fierceness can come back, my tiger side, my golden and black side. You are a tiger, too, and this is why you fight me. But you must understand why I do this. You have no spirit, and so I am giving you my spirit. Because this is the only way you can be pulled to where you can be saved. Because this is the way a mother truly loves her daughter.

Lasso the Alamo

Olga Humphrey

Scene: here and now

Serio-Comic
Tovah: (20s) a Hasidic woman who has recently left her husband

Here, brave Tovah explains why she chose to leave her husband and her community.

TOVAH: Being a woman and a Hasidic Jew is a hard thing. To tell you the truth, I hate gefulte fish. And what did my mother make all the time? Day in, day out, weekdays, weekends, day time, night time, winter, spring, summer and fall? Gefulte fish. I'm thankful I don't have scales and big rubber lips considering how much gefulte fish I ate as a child. You know what else I hate? Stuffed derma, better known as stuffed intestines. Do you know how much stuffed derma I ate…

[KITTY: Dear…]

TOVAH: Oh, sorry. Anyway, I think my life has been similar to Agapi's because we both come from a strong cultural heritage. I never wanted to make myself plain. I wanted to be pretty, but it wasn't something a Hasidic woman could be. We could not be special. But deep inside I knew I was special…I have a confession to make. I never told anybody about this but…I think I loved Tyrone Power more than Schlomo. You may ask: How can you love a dead man? Well, living with Schlomo is like living with a dead man, so if I had to choose—between one dead man and another, I choose Tyrone…I married Schlomo when I was seventeen. I never loved him. There was never any happiness. I watched a lot of television in the afternoon, which I'm not supposed to do. Instead I was supposed to be preparing gefulte fish and stuffed derma…Schlomo's favorite meal. The movies made me dream of other things, other worlds. Schlomo would scold me

45

because I was disobedient. Once when he came home early he caught me watching reruns of Doby Gillis. I really got it for that. I wasn't the perfect wife he wanted. I am scared now, very scared, but maybe I know what it is like to be free for the first time ever...I guess maybe there's one other thing I should tell you. I decided to confront Schlomo, to go back and get my clothes, and tell him I had not been kidnapped but I left of my own free will. I lied. I didn't go back. I realized there was no way to ever go back. I went to the library and wrote him a letter. After I mailed it, I went to two stores: At one I bought a picture frame, at the other I bought a picture of Tyrone Power. I have only two dollars, and I am the happiest woman in the world.

Lasso the Alamo

Olga Humphrey

Scene: here and now

Serio-Comic
Christina: (20s) a woman agonizing over whether or not she should marry her abusive fiancé

> *When her friends intervene in an effort to keep Christina from marrying the man who bit off her nose, the victim offers the following reasons for going through with the nuptials.*

CHRISTINA: No. I was not meant to be the best hula girl. You're trying to make me something I'm not. I have accepted who I am, but it doesn't seem you have. Quite frankly—no pun intended— I am a bimbo. Yes, I am a bimbo and I am proud of it. But I am a nice bimbo. I am a kind person, both to regular women and other bimbos. As a child, I knew that that was what I wanted to be. Other little girls loved Hayley Mills, Judy Garland, Margaret O'Brien. I loved Tuesday Weld, Julie Newmar, Jill St. John and, of course, Ann-Margaret. As a young student, I prayed every night for D's. D cups that is. I don't want to be a liberated woman. Sure, I admire Jane Fonda, but I admired her best in "Barbarella" when she was just a space-age flooze roaming the galaxies in-a French-cut body suit. I have always lived my life for men. In kindergarten I showed my panties to the entire male portion of the class. I kissed my first male in the first grade…in the sandbox after he had peed on himself and I wanted him to feel better. In junior high school, I was known as Frenchie because I was the only girl who knew how to French kiss with pleasure. In high school I was known as Mommie because many young men found comfort in my arms. Do you really know who I am? I have never worn pantyhose because they are not sexy; I have always worn a garter belt. I believe in lip gloss. I believe in red toenails. I believe in teddys. I believe in wearing eyeliner to bed so you don't wake up tired-looking in the morning. But most of all, I believe in love…and love is often full of trials and tribulations…but with discipline and patience, love will always prevail…I do so desperately believe in love…What time is it?

L'Eboueur Sleeps Tonight
(For Worlds Are Destroyed by Day)
Jerome D. Hairston

Scene: here and now

Dramatic
Marilyn: (20–30) an Asian-American prostitute

> *When a regular client, Dookie, proposes, Marilyn offers the violent thug the following refusal.*

MARILYN: You really think it's that easy, don't you?

[DOOKIE: What you mean?]

MARILYN: All this. You got the ring. The papers. Just sign and erase it all. Wash it clean. Be whoever you want me to be. But let me ask you something. How much blood have you seen?

[DOOKIE: What's that got to do with anything?]

MARILYN: It's got to do with your hands. I hear you. Some nights. Water runnin' for hours seems like. But it gets under the nails, don't it? Hides in the cracks. And there ain't no denyin' where they've been. *(Taking off the ring.)* You can't wash it off. Cause it ain't just blood. Or cum. It's too thick. Thick with wickedness. Like ink. That's what it is. Sinners ink. It's how people like you and me, our names get written. Pressed right there on the chest and there ain't no changing the letters. Just gotta live with the stain. You actually think me saying "yes" is gonna change all that?

[DOOKIE: No.]

MARILYN: Then what's the use?

L'Eboueur Sleeps Tonight
(For Worlds Are Destroyed by Day)

Jerome D. Hairston

Scene: here and now

Dramatic
Sue: (39) a semi-worried mother

> *When she notices that her teenaged daughter is missing from the house, Sue wonders how upset she should allow herself to become.*

SUE You think this is all just a dream? Cause somewhere between bedtime and two minutes ago, I got lost. We do have a daughter, right? Isn't that who I bought these for? Three. Three times I looked into that room, but I just don't think there's a daughter under those covers. So, who did I buy these for? God knows I could never sliver into something this size. They have to fit somebody. I'd hate to think I spent fifty dollars putting PJ's on a figment of my imagination...Yes, Hal, Fifty dollars...On Pajamas, yes...Look, the money's not the point, okay. The point is that I know my daughter. Stands about so high. Likes horses. Disney Movies. Wears a size six, and certainly knows better than to ball and toss a brand new set of-PJ's like a pair of dirty socks. So, my question is, if it's not our Amber, then who's out there? Out roaming the two AM streets? Could you please tell me. Cause like I said, I'm at a loss, Hal. I really am. At a total loss.

Lions, Tigers and Bears
Michael P. Scassera

Scene: here and now

Serio-Comic
Judy: (30s) a victim of the sexless '90s

> *Judy bemoans the repression of sexuality rampant in our age and longs for the comfort of companionship. Here, she describes an unsavory experience she recently had at a party.*

JUDY: I forced myself to go to this party recently. An amazing shit party, if you know what I mean. This was a big step for me, really, because I've come to absolutely hate parties. Whenever I get into social situations, I find that people, as a general group, irritate the shit out of me.

> [RAY: I think about a year from now. Ten years, twenty years. And I still see myself buying microwaveable entrees for one. Owning a cat or a parrot or some other small, useless animal. I see myself living alone in a cold water flat...which really concerns me because I have no idea what the hell a cold water flat is.]

JUDY: For me, parties have become these pointless gatherings of lying, fucked-up people. And there's always this particularly irritating bitch who stands off from the crowd, you know the type. Waiting for people to dare speak with her, looking down on everyone else, tying to make her own insecurities seem somehow attractive. But I started to go to parties again when I realized that I was, in fact, this bitch of whom I complain.

> [RAY: What happens to people who end up alone? They usually end up a little crazy, don't they? Either that or they end up one of those people who goes around saying, *My work is the most important thing in my life.* A concept that is a little

hard to swallow if one is a customer service representative for A.T.&T.]

JUDY: Well, in an effort to be terribly bold, I go to this amazing shit party. Well, to start with, everything in this couple's apartment is mauve, and I have this thing about mauve. It makes me anxious. But I'm managing to keep myself together. I saunter over to the buffet table and I see these little things that look like homemade chocolates, only they are definitely not chocolate. But I throw caution to the wind and try one. Well, I end up chewing on this thing for like ten minutes because it tastes like rubber but I can't spit it out because some yuppie bimbo approaches and within seconds starts telling me the story of how she contracted vaginal herpes from a toilet seat at Tavern on the Green.

[RAY: It seems to me that this fear of being alone has recently reached epidemic proportions. No matter how bad I get to feeling about my own situation, though, I always feel a little bit better when I see other people who are clearly more pathetic and more desperate for connection than I. It makes me feel better.]

JUDY: Once this idiot finally finishes her herpes saga, I turn my head real fast and spit this disgusting little chocolate-like thing into my hand and I'm standing there with no idea where to toss this brown blob, but then this really sweet guy comes over and hands me a mauve napkin. Well, when I politely asked the hostess what this thing was was she tells me…brace yourself…she tells me it's a duck's heart. I was gnawing for ten minutes on a heart!

[RAY: For an example of someone more pathetic than I, I refer to a party I attended recently. I was just sitting back, observing the scene, when I began to focus on this awkward woman who was eating a sautéed duck heart. It's clear to me that this woman wants to spit the thing out, but she was too embarrassed thinking someone would see her.]

JUDY: It was absolutely revolting! I would have suspected as much before, but I found out then that hearts are clearly indigestible.

The Maiden's Prayer

Nicky Silver

Scene: NYC

Dramatic
Libby: (20–30) a young woman whose life has bottomed-out

> *When Taylor, the man she loves, marries her sister, Libby*
> *thinks her life is pretty lousy until she loses her job and finds*
> *that it's worse than lousy. Just when things couldn't get*
> *worse for this recovering alcoholic, they do, as she here,*
> *describes.*

LIBBY: Well, I thought, I'll do what Paul does. I'll anesthetize myself by having anonymous sex continually with a series of nameless, faceless strangers.

[PAUL: I don't do that—]

LIBBY: Oh wake up and smell the coffee. I'm not judging, by the way. It's my nature, yes, but in this instance what do I care if you fuck and suck your way to the hall of fame. Just as long as you're safe. You are safe, aren't you?

[PAUL: Perfectly.]

LIBBY: So I put on my sexiest black dress and went to the bar on my corner. I thought it was tasteful. I thought I looked classy! *(She removes her raincoat revealing a black cocktail dress of dubious taste, in which she, indeed looks very sexy.)* Apparently I've lost touch with the popular aesthetic.

[PAUL: It's very…nice.]

LIBBY: Can you believe I paid five hundred dollars for this dress? I had a job at the time. So, I'm sitting at the bar drinking my club soda, having turned over the leaf of sobriety, and the seconds are dragging by like hours and no one talks to me. And I wish I were dead. I'm feeling sorry myself all over. I mean what do I have? Who do I have?

[PAUL: You have me.]

LIBBY: Well you're not enough!! I'm sorry, but we're friends and it would be different if I hadn't known Taylor, if I hadn't been in love, if I hadn't felt, really, the kind of love from novels, from Bronte novels and teenaged songs. But I did and now I just feel sick! I feel sick and full of some kind of poison all the time!!

[PAUL: What happened!?]

LIBBY: Well, I'm sitting at the bar, getting older and older, and then, finally, this guy, this older guy, he offers to buy me a drink. I think, jackpot, fabulous. So I have a stinger. Then another…His name is Jack. He's gotta be sixty. And if he weighs an ounce he tips the scales at three bills. He's big. But he seems perfectly nice. And I'm glad to have the drink. And, believe it or not, I'm glad that he's talking and I don't have to be entertaining or charming or anything. I can just sit and drink and listen. He's divorced. Two kids. In the security business and I'm sure he's a nice person. I'm sure he's a perfectly fine human being…but, um… *(She's finding it difficult to talk.)* …Eventually he asks me if I'll go back to his apartment. And I think of you, and I think of Taylor, and I don't really answer, I don't say anything. I just nod. His apartment is fine. All the furniture looks like it's rented. Everything matches like a room in a department store. There are pictures of his children on the bookcase. A boy and a girl who stare smiling at us the whole time. And he takes off my coat and he's mumbling quietly that I'm beautiful… *(She is trying not to cry.)* …and I'm trying to enjoy it…because it's nice to be told. And we go to the bed room and he loosens his tie and unzips my dress. He turns off the light so I can't see his body. And he puts his hand on my shoulder, which doesn't feel bad, moving my hair and kisses my collar bone, and then my breast, and makes sounds. And then he kisses my mouth and my eyes are closed so I'm somewhere else, with someone else, with Taylor. And then this man, this Jack, this divorced father of two puts me on the bed and climbs on top of me and we have sex…and the horrible thing of it is…I didn't mind. I didn't care. It wasn't pleasant or ugly or thrilling or awful. It was nothing. It was just…brief.

54

[PAUL: Well—]

LIBBY: And then he turned on the light. He grabbed his bathrobe and ran, afraid I would see him, into the bathroom. I got dressed. And when he came out he was dressed. "Do you want a ride home?" I nodded. And then, he walked toward me. And when he reached me he put one hand on my neck and pulled my head towards his until our lips touched. And while he kissed me, with his other hand, he found my hand, and he put, in my hand, three, folded, one hundred dollar bills...And then he whispered thank you.

[PAUL: God.]

LIBBY: I wasn't, really, insulted.

[PAUL: *(Holding her.)* Oh my God.]

LIBBY: *(Crying.)* I was grateful.

[PAUL: My God.]

LIBBY: I was grateful.

[PAUL: It's okay.]

LIBBY: I was glad for the money.

Marcus is Walking

Joan Ackerman

Scene: the simplest possible car

Serio-Comic
Caitlin: (30s) a woman prone to panic attacks while driving

> *Caitlin suffers from crippling panic attacks when she drives on the Mass Pike. Here, she drives onto the dreaded highway to test the response time of her new beau.*

CAITLIN: *(Chattily, merrily, thoroughly enjoying herself.)* I'm not going to do just fine, I tell you that right now. I'm going to freak out. I haven't been back here in two years. Not since it happened. Now it takes me six hours to drive to Boston on back roads instead of two and a half. Did you know that one out of eight women have panic attacks? One out of eight. That's a lot of panic. I know it's psychological at this point. I know it's all in my head but I can't control it, ooo, could you take your hand off my thigh please. I like your hand, it's just a little distracting. It's like the road freezes in a freeze frame, things stop moving as a video, and my mind jams into this…ozone…*warp* and it's *exhausting* like I'm towing the car with my brain and I can't breathe and I get disconnected from my body and I think I'll pass out. I never *have* passed out but I think I will. If there's a breakdown lane, it doesn't happen; if there isn't one, it's…god, it's indescribably awful. Zack, could you please stop chewing on my ear; it's kind of noisy. Maybe you'd like to come by later. *(She can't believe her audacity.)* The weird thing, I'm more afraid of the fear than I am of actually getting into a car crash.

> [ZACK: *(Pulling back from her.)* It's not going to happen again. You're over it.]

CAITLIN: *(Still chatty, still buoyantly happy.)* I'm not over it. You're going to have to take the wheel at some point. You know it's recently occurred to me, maybe it's not so strange, to have a panic attack in this situation. Maybe something in my brain knows something I don't know; maybe it's protecting me and being very sensible, very rational. I mean, up until this century human beings didn't go faster than, what, five miles an hour, unless they were flung up on an ox or a horse or something, pitched out a castle window. For centuries, for millennia, humans have traveled very, very slowly. When you think about it, going sixty miles an hour, going *forty* miles an hour is a profoundly *unnatural* thing to do. *Insanely* dangerous. Maybe some part of my brain realizes this and says what the fuck are you doing out in this little tinny shitty metal box that can crumple like gum foil in an instant, flying, hurtling through space alongside of hundreds of other people in little tinny metal boxes many of whom are complete idiots, people who willingly kept Reagan in office for eight years, *morons* entrusted with these death machines simply by virtue of having passed a multiple choice test they can take over and over and over until they pass? It's insane. Really, people have panic attacks in very logical places—elevators, airplanes, cars—dangerous places. Maybe it's not panic, maybe it's preservation of the species, common sense, it's "Get your body out of here. This is a very, very *stupid* place for you to be."

[ZACK: *(Nervous now.)* Hmm.]

CAITLIN: You know it's curious, they say money and sex are the key issues in a relationship. I think driving is more important; a couple's dynamic in a car. A car is more of a hotbed for emotions than a bed. I could never go out with a bad driver. I have broken up with guys because they're horrible drivers. If I'm going to be happy with a man I have to feel like I can lie down and put my head on his lap while he's at the wheel and not worry; not worry that he's not watching the road closely, not concentrating. I have to feel secure that he's driving competently, *defensively.* Give me safety points on a guy's driving record over Kurt Russell's thighs any day. Okay, we're getting close. There's a stretch up here very soon; no break down lane, a long monotonous guard rail, pressing in from the side, oppressive, looming, encroaching, dominating, paralyzing, you ready?

Marla's Devotion

Linda Eisenstein

Scene: here and now

Dramatic
Marla: (30s) a woman seeking to change her life

> *Marla has recently begun to engage in systematic prostra-*
> *tion—not unlike Buddhist pilgrims—in an effort to know her*
> *spiritual self. Here, she offers some observations regarding*
> *the concept of devotion.*

MARLA: Devotion. Devotion is a very powerful thing. There's nothing weak or passive about it. I mean, look at nuns and monks.
They're tough cookies. Catholics, Buddhists, Hindus. They go to
bare rooms ringed with flame and soft pungent smells, sit on
their heels and quiet their mind. There can be sounds all around,
the rush of the world—screeching tires, slamming doors, even
machine-gun bursts—but they still can go to this quiet place of
Devotion. Where their hearts can open and fill with love. Where
they can feel the universe pouring love in their direction. I'll bet
they become like magnets in their bare rooms—a lodestone so
charged that all the good energy in the world runs their way, like
a river or a fountain. They pull it to them on their breath, and it
gets supercharged and magnified inside them and then they
breathe it out. And the wind carries their devotion through the
air like spores that float out over the city. And for a split second,
there is no pain in the world. Boy oh boy. I'd like to learn how to
breathe like that. Even once. Boy oh boy. I sure would.

Molly's Delicious

Craig Wright

Scene: an apple orchard in Pine City, MN. Autumn, 1965

Serio-Comic
Alison: (18) a young woman on the verge of motherhood

> *The father of Alison's baby has shipped out for Vietnam, leav-*
> *ing her unwed and in the lurch. When her well-meaning aunt*
> *sets her up with Alec, a somber young mortician who has*
> *loved her from afar, Alison does her best to be the earnest*
> *young man's friend.*

ALISON: These apples are all Molly's Delicious. This apple grower in
Wisconsin, way way back before World War I, "developed" it, I
guess, as a tribute to Molly, the girl of his dreams. He took a
branch from a Red Delicious and grafted it onto a Keepsake, and
after two years of trial and error, created this apple with the high-
est sugar content of any apple ever grown in America. And with
a basket of those apples, the first Molly's Delicious picked from
the first crop ever, he showed up at her door and proposed. No
one believes in love like that anymore, Alec. No one!

[ALEC: I do.]

ALISON: I do too. But nobody else does, you know? They've all
given up and they want us to give up too, because our faith
reminds them of their failures, which they want to forget. Isn't
that sick? It's so sick. I want you to know I'm not mad at you,
Alec, I don't blame *you* for glumping out here and pestering me,
I know it wasn't your idea. The way I see it, you're just like me,
we're in this together. We're two young people with natural
dreams who are about to be fed into a giant crunching gearbox
because nobody can stand to have us around if our hearts aren't
broken. Do you know what I mean?

[ALEC: I do.]

ALISON: I know you do, Alec, because you're a good person. That's the only reason I'm out here with you, I could tell right away you were a good person, and I didn't want to let their sick, secret plan rob us of our chance to be friends, you know, because we deserve it. We of all people should get something out of this stupid situation, just to show them, you know? Just to remind them where it's at. Alec, I have more hope and imagination in my little finger than the whole ugly world put together, do you know what that's like?

[ALEC: No.]

ALISON: It's really lonely.

The Names of the Beast

Linda Eisenstein

Scene: here and now

Serio-Comic
Alicia: (30–40) a novelist and academic on the verge of a melt-down

> *Years of frustration have led Alicia to quit writing. She has invited her inner circle of sister scribes to participate in the ritualistic destruction of her work via fire. When someone suggests that Alicia needs to accept change in her life she makes the following reply.*

ALICIA: Change? Every time someone talks about change it just translates into more work. I've read advice columns until they're coming out my ass. I should do yoga. I should eat natural foods. I should pick up rocks and twigs and sacred buttons and sew them into a dream pillow. Make a dream pillow? For Christ's sake, I don't have any dreams. I can't remember a single one. I don't sleep long enough to dream. All I do is run all day. Then I come home and I run. And then I hear all this stupid advice on how I'm supposed to be doing more things. Well, all I see is things getting added to my schedule. Nothing ever gets taken away. So I'm going to take something away, goddamn it. I'm going to take this away. I'm tired of having this thing, label, expectation, hanging over my head. It's over! It's done. When I don't have time to dream—bam, that's it.

Noah's Archives

Stephen Spoonamore

Scene: a bar

Serio-Comic
Nebekenezer: (30–40) a barkeep

> *On a dark and stormy night, Nebekenezer regales the denizens of her saloon with a colorful take on the Biblical Noah.*

NEBEKENEZER: Fuck Adam and Eve. Fuck'em. The whole things a sham…Tree of knowledge…yum fucking yum…And there's Adam "Yo! Rib, Like Sup with that!" And she's "ooh oops honey God said don't? but the serpent said it was…" Giggle Giggle, Like what, ever. Adam the fucking loser was already on his second wife. Lilith. Oh stuff it. Every time you bring up Lilith you get some chick who went to women's college, or should have, getting that "Go Girls, Go Girls, chick power thing in their eyes and Let me tell you it's fucking booh-big-fucking no way bogus. Chick's sell each other out so fucking fast. Not like guys. No way. They stick together. They will lie and cheat and scam you but they will stick together while they go. They got a code about that built into their wiring…chicks…fuck…shit hits the fan and they sell each other down the river, trading in as fast as they can for the best chunk of provider or meat or stud hunk around. I see it every night. Every fucking night. I hate it. I'm one of em. God I am going to puke if I think about it any more. Okay…so fucking Adam and Eve and all that La-dee-dah about paradise. Bullshit. Adam and Lilith had paradise in the real bible, the one before the medieval editors got it, and she got a little wrinkly, or a little sure of herself or whatever and walked on that asshole…he clearly already was into the knowledge fruit himself, and I bet hitting it with Lilith, which would explain her leaving, and God said, "Woah, dude, sucks! Total Bummer!" They stick together, like nothing we can equal. "Let me Snake a rib from you and give me a seck and" Tadah!!! The perfect compliant beach bimbo! "Dude, and we'll pretend the tree of knowledge is bad for her, hee hee." Fucking stick together every time. I am so far off what I meant to tell you...I mean the Smith College wanabee over there is thinking, "well were the descendants of Lilith...la la la..." Bull fucking shit, and Yes I saw you checking out ass when you came in,...You're forgetting the fucking flood!!!!! Noah!!!! We are all descended from Noah! Who was from the dumb ass sell out Adam/Eve side of the early human tree. So who are we? I'll tell you children of Noah...He builds a boat, an ark...twenty cubits by forty cubits...a cubit is about the size of an '82 Buick Electra, making the fucking thing about the size of the parking lot at 25rd and 6th where they have that great flea market every weekend...another place to go watch chicks sell each other out...fuck...sorry...So he stuffs all the animals in the world in this thing. You think the restrooms in most clubs are gross? And then it rains for forty and forty, everything gets moist, and then floats around for a couple a years, eating what? It's a little uncertain, fish?, and then runs into a mountain top. Okay. Bible study class. What did Noah do when He landed? Anyone...Shit...come on... what would you do? He rejoiced! Then those fucking medieval editors claim he gave thanks to god, but who knows, I mean they stick together, I am personally skeptical, then and they didn't edit this out...he planted a vineyard, he and his sons oh yea, and their wives, beget children and he raised cattle fowl and a garden. In that order! Fuck the thanks...they wooped it up, first thing he did—planted grapes, because they needed a fucking drink like you could not believe! And then got laid. That's who we are! The rest is just...Fluff! And You Don't have to plant the grapes! You can just come in here and say to me! I NEED A DRINK LIKE NOAH! Because we are all descended from that old lush and the giggle chicks he and his sons picked up down the line from Adam and Eve! Don't get me started...just listen to your ancestors...rejoice children of Noah! Suck the Grape! Fuck one another...It's who we are...

Noah's Archives
Stephen Spoonamore

Scene: a bar

Serio-Comic
Buns: (20–30) a.k.a. Judith, a temp/actress obsessed with her body

> *Here, a woman who has extended lots of time and energy on making her body perfect reveals her hatred of men.*

BUNS: I have spent so much money on underwear and for what? What? Losers…LOO-OO-OOsers! A couple of years ago I was looking and I was really looking too? And I was looking so fine! I'd just dumped this tre-way-ultra-seismic Loo-oozer boy and said…Girlfriend…You are going to the gym and you are going to tone it all for you…you are going to be the body queen for no one other than yourself body queen! Body Queen #1 body queen for the day and not for any Man at all…none…you need another loser boy like you need crabs…which…but…anyway…So I did. I was like EVERY DAY! 5:30!, At the Gym!…me!…go girl! Go Girl! Work it!…working it…working it hard too, not like fucking spinning on downhill…I am talking about machines…stairmasters at insane incline levels! I am talking free weights and box step…Reps? Reps!? I was Reps! And I am talking I was there every day for two months…Every every day…I was that woman who is at the gym and the other women all came in thinking "There's that bitch who is ALWAYS here." Hah! Hah! HAAAA! and they would give me that look like they do when you are always there an they can not do anything but look at your ass and just weep that they are fucking losers, stuck fucking losers, with flabby ass asses, who miss out on that ass because I am there every day and they are not…HAAAA!!! I am lucky that I didn't get hurt or anything you are not supposed to do that I could have gotten a stress fracture or something like that...but I was lucking and and lucky and I didn't and I was...so fucking tight...Firm! Nothing moved!...see how nice it is now...see that movement...I had none! Nothing Nothing moved unless I moved it!...I was fucking Buns of steel...Long lines pieces of wire, pure tone buns of steel, and I went to go buy some of the underwear you only dare to wear when you are and I fucking rocked it! I rocked it so hard...I made myself fucking...my nipples dance in the stuff...the best lace edges...nothing control anything...control! hah! I was control...Deeeeeee!...So there it was lace to get wet about and my iron ass underneath it and the thing you start thinking about is...like...Why? *(A pause.)* And then I figured I would get out there again and this is when I was looking, and Like I had like not looked at all for like ever...and I am like I do not need another loser to ruin this...No loser gets this! So I come off this insane gym faze...I was like...deeeeeeeeeeeee...just this gym lazer... deeeeeeeee...but now...I got this underwear and I was...Like Daaaaaaaah. Like Daaaaa,...Deeee...Daaaaah-ah...I was masturbating every night...I would work out Deeeeeeeeee... and then put on this underwear an I would just... Daaaaahaaaahhaaa. I would sometimes just go nuts on myself...I have this vibrator...another...LOOzer bought me once as like a joke...and I am like...yeesh!...but then for like the first time since he was buh-bye-bye I got the thing out and...I bought the batteries from the guy on the train one dollah one dollah one dollah, boattree one dalloh...and I...fucking wore it out...wore it out...Daaaaaa, DAAAAAA daaaaaa...batteries every day...I mean it adds up...like a pack a day smoking habit...you gotta... So then every single guy is looking good...I mean, And I am looking like a million dollars and every night I am working myself longer and longer and I just...you'd think it would have satisfied things, but it was backward...every day I wanted the real thing more...more and more and more...I am liking checking out guys I barely know, then guys I don't know and wondering if I can just walk up to them and just...bam! DAAAAAAAAAAA!...and you start thinking about it so much it gets in the way of your life...And the voice in

65

here saying "NO LOOOOOOSZERS!" got to be like "no losers"…
got to be like…" "…and so I went out with this guy who a
friend…knew…He never knew what hit him… DAAAAAAAA-
AAAAAA! Fucking…I loved fucking that night like no night
before or since…He was like a living breathing warm thing and
the batteries don't wear out…I mean they do…but I recharged
him…I loved it. I even loved him…I fuck…and he never called
again…fucking loser…didn't even notice my underwear…liked
my ass though…said so…fucking losers. Loo-oo-ooo-oozers. All
of them… *(Women Hate Men song.)*

The Northern Lights

Lauren McConnell

Scene: a beat-up old car heading north to Canada

Dramatic
Kelsey: (22) a young woman on the verge of ending a relationship

> *Kelsey has been living with Zephyr in an isolated cabin in Canada. Following a visit home to California, Kelsey no longer wants to rough-it in the woods. Here, she prepares to give Zephyr the bad news.*

KELSEY: I want to go home. I want to catch a bus tomorrow and go home.

[ZEPHYR: We're going home!]

KELSEY: To California! I can't go back to the cabin and the goat and the smell! Not after California!

[ZEPHYR: You want to leave?]

KELSEY: I can't take it anymore! I'm sorry! I've just begun to realize that, I don't know, I just want a normal life. I didn't think I did, but I do.

[ZEPHYR: Our life isn't *that* strange. It's just simple.]

KELSEY: Zephyr, everything *about* our life is strange! You've just lived up here so long you don't see it anymore. Even *I* didn't *really* see it until we went to visit my parents! We live in a house with no electricity! That is strange. The only time I get to hear music is in the car! Sometimes I sneak out to the car just to listen to the radio—even if it is nothing but this country western shit! And our bathtub is outside the house! That is strange. How many people have to put on snow boots every time they want to take a bath? How many people have to milk a fucking goat every time they need a little cream for their coffee? We live a strange life! But the strangest thing of all is we don't *have* to live this way! We have options! We could move and get *real* jobs and have a normal life. Our parents are even willing to help us! But instead we choose to live like the Beverly Hillbillies before they struck oil. Normal people don't live like that! Normal people don't *want* to live like that.

[ZEPHYR: You used to like it.]

KELSEY: I'm growing up fast. I remember how we used to sit around complaining about California—about the building, the growth, the polluted, modern rat-race. *We* knew a better way. *We* were better than *all* of *them*. We would live in harmony with nature. We were so self-righteous! I'll tell you this much: I *enjoyed* being in California. I liked the weather. I liked the malls! I liked the freeways! I *liked* it!

Polaroid Stories

Naomi Iizuka

Scene: a pier at the edge of the city. The late 1990s, night

Dramatic
Eurydice: (18–20) a young woman wandering through the under-world

As she crosses the River of Forgetfulness, Eurydice tells Orpheus and Persephone of her compelling need to forget.

EURYDICE: you look like someone who knows how it goes, so i'm going to tell you how it goes,
i'm high, right, and this guy
he says to me, where are you from—bitch—
he wants to touch me, get inside of me, know everything about me.
he wants to know how i got all these scars on my pretty little body.
i tell him, sweet as i know how: baby, i forget.
i drink from the river of forgetfulness.
i forget the names i forget the faces i forget the stories i forget all kinds of shit.
when he's asleep, i roll him, i kick his ass, take his cash, take his fancy watch
and i'm looking at him
and all i can think is
who are you to me,
like you know me
like you think i'm going to tell you the truth
like you think i'm going to give you that—
yeah, baby, i got scars
i got scars all over, but i don't even know their story, see.
ain't no story, cause i forget.

Polaroid Stories

Naomi Iizuka

Scene: a pier at the edge of the city. The late 1990s, night

Dramatic
Persephone: (20s) A woman teetering on the edge

Rage and grief over the loss of her son have driven Persephone to trash a public restroom.

PERSEPHONE: yeah yeah yeah, fuckin song sung blue—tss. so what do you want to know about me, cause i'll tell you everything, right, i got a thousand stories to tell, and i'll tell them for free, i'll fuckin give them away. so what it is, right, i had a baby. he ain't with me now or anything. i gave him up. i was pretty messed up at the time, but that's a whole nother story. when he was born, my baby, he had something wrong with his heart, with the way his heart was put together—fuck, i don't know. it's been so long, you know, i forget. anyway it ain't like i think about him everyday or anything—it ain't even like that. just sometimes, i think about where he is now, you know, and what he looks like, if he looks like me, if he remembers me, stupid shit like that.
(Echo comes upon Persephone, she notices Echo, looking at her in the mirror.)
PERSEPHONE: yeah, what are you looking at? i see you looking at me, like you got some kind of problem, you got a problem? what the hell are you looking at? you want to piss me off, bitch? you better get out of my face before i kick your ass, cause i ain't none of your business to be looking at—what are you looking at, huh, what the fuck are you looking at—
(Echo goes. Persephone gazes at her reflection, and slowly turns to stone.)

Private Eyes

Steven Dietz

Scene: here and now

Dramatic
Lisa: (30s) an actress who is having an affair with her director

> *Lisa has been sleeping with Adrian, a Brit who is directing her
> and her husband, Matthew, in a new play. Here, Lisa reveals
> her overwhelming feelings of fear and guilt to a therapist.*

LISA: *(Urgently.)* I had a dream last night—

   [FRANK: Tell me, Lisa.]

LISA: And in my dream I am washing dishes. I have taken off my
wedding ring, as I always do. And I reach into the soapy water
and pull out a little Tupperware container. And I remove the top.
And there is a *heart* inside. A human heart, still beating. And in
the dream I remember reading that a heart can live for about five
hours outside the body before it dies—

   [FRANK: Between four and six hours, actually, depending on
   age, condition—]

LISA: And I know that before it dies I have to find out who it
belongs to—and return it to him. So, I seal it up in the
Tupperware. And I get in my car. I go to Adrian's hotel room. I
open the door. I reach inside his chest…and his heart is there,
pounding away. So, I drive home. And I look everywhere for
Matthew. I drive to rehearsal. I check the restaurant, the book
store, the deli. I can't find him anywhere. I go home and wait for
him. I sit on the floor and stare at my watch…holding the little
container in my hands…the heart beating…the hours ticking
away…

Reading the Mind of God

Pat Gabridge

Scene: Benatek Castle, near Prague. 1600

Serio-Comic Dramatic
Barbara Kepler: (25) a short-tempered, melancholy woman once married to a wealthy merchant and now married to a penniless—through brilliant astronomer

> *Barbara's new husband, Johannes Kepler, has been invited to join Tycho Brahe at Benatek Castle. When Barbara and the children finally arrive she finds the environment of the scientists not at all to her liking as she here reports.*

BARBARA: Johan, you must speak to Christine. They won't give me any cloth. I need to make new clothes for the girls, they're living in rags. And that is the least of my concerns about the children. The things that they are exposed to in this house, the immorality. Coarse language, debauchery, sorcery. Some say Tycho is a sorcerer. He is certainly a buffoon. Loud. Why is everyone in this house so loud? And why are they especially loud when we're reading our prayer service? They're heathens, Johan. Heathens. And that Jep, well he just frightens me. What can you expect when the house is headed by an unmarried couple. Sinful! That Christine, I'm sure she seems nice to you. She likes you. But she's constantly short with me. Rude. I should not have to suffer so. Why did we come here? I want to go back to Graz, Johan. This country is filled with disease. The Plague has killed thousands in Prague. Filth. They wallow in filth. I have developed an ache in my back. I can barely stand. We need a new mattress. Ours is so worn, we might as well sleep on bare wood. Are you listening to me, Johan? Are you listening to me? I want to go home. Do you hear me?

Scared of Demons

Michael Steffens-Moran

Scene: here and now

Dramatic
Woman: (30–40) a woman remembering her mythic and frightening childhood

Here, a woman whose childhood was defined by her intense fear of demons (courtesy of the over-active imagination of her Sunday School teacher and a stolen glance at The Exorcist*) here describes a scene from her past that foreshadowed endless nights of terror.*

WOMAN: I'm seven years old. It's breakfast. Mother's reading the newspaper and she looks up and she says about these people, um, these people who look out of their eyes sideways—like this—and say things like: "Hey, you wanna piece of candy, little girl?" And by just the way she says it I can tell that she's talking about those people that live in alleys and only come out at night—all black and spooky, or skinny and really pale. See, and sometimes they go out after dark, driving in these long black cars with dark windows, and they look for little girls. Cuz I guess they like to eat 'em. And maybe they'd say, "Hey, little girl, wanna ride?" Christine wants to know if they'd make us eat the candy. She's so dumb. And Mother says, "A bad person will lie, a bad person always lies, they'll tell you that their candy's alright. But candy from strangers could have razor blades and sand burrs stuck inside. So never, never talk to strangers." And Daddy makes that toot-sound with his lips when Mother's done talking and he says: "If you don't know their name, don't take nothing from them, don't talk to them. Savvy? They take you away, make you do things little girls shouldn't. Make you not our little girls anymore." And that scares me in a funny way so I hug my Daddy really hard. And Daddy laughs, like he's saying: "I'll never let them take you, kiddo. I'll protect my little girl." And then Mother says, "that's enough of that," and tells me to go get dressed for Sunday school.

Scotland Road

Jeffrey Hatcher

Scene: a white room, the present

Dramatic
Winnifred: (20–30) a young woman claiming to have been aboard the Titanic

> *When Winnifred is discovered floating on an iceberg in the North Atlantic and dressed in late nineteenth century clothes, the only word she utters to her rescuers is: Titanic. A mysterious and seemingly wealthy man named John has Winnifred brought to Maine where he and a doctor endeavor to discover the truth about her origins. At first, John claims to be a great-grandson of John Jacob Astor, an American millionaire who went down with the overly famous ship. Winnifred eventually reveals that she knows his true identity and here describes the first time she ever met John aboard a certain ship, many years ago...without Leonardo and Kate romping on the foredecks.*

WINNIFRED: The first time I saw him was at the third class staircase. Sunday morning worship. Feeling the eyes across the room during the hymn and the admonition. And then the eyes meeting. A hat tipped. An offer of a walk along the deck on a Sunday afternoon. And then a spot of tea. And then supper. And more. And the questions. "What do you do before bed, darlin'?" "I read the Bible. And then—sometimes—my "Strand." But on Sunday, just the Bible." And you know how they keep us in third class. Men on one end, women on the other. Like we were children, and they who run the ship know better. But you can come from one end to the other. You can come down from high *above* as well. And it's dark out. And the sea and the sky and the stars have gone by. And indeed there is the Bible. Laid out on the blanket.

75

Across my breast. Unopened. And the "Strand" even farther away. And the rap on the door then comes. And, yes, a talk would be lovely, although it's not really proper in the room. "Oh, I am going to work in the household of Mrs. George Haverland Coe of Pittsburgh, Pennsylvania. In-service just like yourself, but I could never claim a position as fancy as you. To be in service to such a fine family, I am very impressed indeed to be sure." And then more talk. And laughter, very hushed and silent. And then the question. And the question again. And again. And then an answer. And the Bible is placed aside near the "Strand." And then, in the dark, in the silence, in the murmur of the machines in the heart of the ship, a finger draws along the side…and wakes. "It's the ghost of your aunt, Mrs. James, wagging a finger at her naughty niece." And I laugh. And we go on. And then there is another knock on the door. And voices in the passageway. "We should go up and see…" "No, darlin', not yet." "We should go up and see what it is…" "No, not yet. A little longer, darlin'. A little longer." But I want to see what it is, and I look out the porthole. And it is a sea of ice, mountains of ice going by, so beautiful in such a calm, black sea. We've stopped, and we can look out at this beautiful field of ice. "Let's go up," I say. "Let's go up and see." But we don't. "Listen to me, darlin'. I must go up to the master, or there'll be hell to pay. But I'll come back. You wait under the covers, and when I come back I'll take you up to see the ice. I know a way to get up to the first class Promenade Deck where we can see, and no one will know. I know a way up through a central passageway, a passageway that runs all the way through the length of the ship, from bow to stern. The officers call it 'Park Lane.' The crew calls it 'Scotland Road.' We'll go up, we'll go up all the way on 'Scotland Road.'. And I'll show you the ice, I'll show you the mountains of ice. I'll take you up 'Scotland Road.'" "Take me up. Take me up! *Take me all the way to the Hebrides!*" He was so beautiful. My handsome valet to the Astors. He never came back. *(She stares out front.)*

Singing the Bones

Caitlin Hicks

Scene: here and now

Dramatic
Meg: (40s) a compassionate midwife who's seen it all

Here, Meg shares a story about her father, a preacher man.

MEG: Can I tell you something? About the last time I saw my Daddy? My Daddy was a big man. He was the preacher. The thing about my Daddy is, whenever he's in a room, there's this space he takes up. Like he's already breathed in all of the air and when that air was inside him he gave it a sermon and told it how to behave. So when he breathes out, it's already reverent air. And when you inhale it and exhale it, it transforms into this Mist of Reverence that fills up every corner of the room. And the sun shines through the window like grace from heaven and every molecule is holding itself waiting for my Daddy to speak. And when he speaks, it is the word of the Lord! The last time I saw him, he had a green dress on. He was in an oxygen tent on his back with a tube in his nose. I was all shaky anticipation' him cause I knew he'd been through a dreadful thing, and sure enough his eyes were closed, I had to look for his breath by watching his chest move up and down. And it was so still in that room I could taste it. I contributed to it! The promise of God like we were all in a church. And my eyes wandered around the room, looking for some powerful distraction and right there, pinned under his butt was his bible! And like a shot, my heart went out to him. A little thing like that! His bible! Like he was afraid and he had been praying for himself! I felt like the forgiving Lord in that moment! And then I remembered the song I sang to myself on the bed every day of being a girl, a song I never sang out loud. I grabbed Daddy's hand like it was going to save me. All the veins thick and raised, I remembered that hand. I turned it over, of course it was the same hand I knew! Whatever that hand had done, it was familiar. It was my father's hand. I knew what to expect from it. Then I saw his leg, jagged with huge staples like the inseam of a pair of stockings all the way up to his crotch. Just then Daddy moved, his gown fell off and just like that, I was looking at his penis and his balls! Right there, soft and shriveled, hiding between his legs, but out in the open, just the same. The Doctor was right behind me. He saw it too. His hand went up. Instinctively I froze; it was a habit of mine. Then the doctor went past me and covered up my Daddy! So he wouldn't be embarrassed because his balls were showing. And he did it with purpose, like it had to be done before anything else. Like it was his duty to save my Daddy, The Preacher, from that humiliation! Oh, my mind filled up with pictures then. Daddy died the next day during no visiting hours.

Singing the Bones

Caitlin Hicks

Scene: here and now

Dramatic
Nicole: (37) a pregnant woman who desperately wants to give birth at home

Here, determined Nicole tells her midwife why she wants to deliver her twins at home, even if it means risking her babies' lives.

NICOLE: You are asking me the question that you have been afraid to ask me all these months. You are telling me that if I don't go to the hospital there is a chance that my babies will not be alive when the birth is over. You want to know if I am willing to risk that my babies will die? I understand this so clearly. I am the mother of these children. My natural instinct requires me to want them to survive with every cell of my body. As a mother, this is my only desperation.

You have asked me in the past, what I bring to this birth? And I have not told you the full story. And now is the time to tell you. What happened was that I was alone, the father of my second child was in another land when it was my time to deliver. But I felt myself lucky to have made the friendship of the Doctor January, who became the main man in my life, and secretly I put all my desires on him. He was the only one there for me. He knew I hated the hospital, and so he agreed to give me an exam in exchange for a foot massage at his home once a month. What's wrong with that? He thought it was okay, so I relaxed. His wife would fix a vegetarian meal, and I would massage his feet, and he would make sure everything with the pregnancy was going fine.

I was one week overdue the night he invite me for dinner. His wife was at a business meeting in Vancouver. He brought some wine and he said, "You know your problem is you're too nervous about this, you gotta lighten up, have a glass of wine, relax, we're going to have a nice time here." So we did. And while I was massaging his feet he say, "Forgive me, Nicole, for what I am about to do." And he pull up my dress and put his penis inside of me. "I'm sorry," he say, when he finish, "I couldn't help myself, you are so beautiful."

I was so confused! To hear him say to me that I am beautiful, well, these are words a woman likes to hear! But I didn't give him permission to do that! It was something he took for himself because he could see that it would be easy to have.

And just like that my labour began. And this time it was moving through me and I was very high with it, I was handling it I was feeling in control. And so I drive myself home, because I need to be alone in a safe place. And I don't know how much time go by, I was moving with the earth, rumbling and quaking and making a lot of noise. When the telephone ring, I felt certain that the baby was going to be born! My girlfriend Odile was there in a few moments, with a taxi to get me to the hospital. And then something strange happen. When I see the door to the hospital, there is a memory of the aluminum, the smell of the hallway, a recognition. I am suddenly a teenager again, afraid of the pain and captive in my body, remembering the strangers around me and my humiliation. And all of a sudden, the work my body was doing turned to pain. Only this time it is worse, with things stuck into every opening in my body and taped to me, I can hardly move. The time passes, interrupted always by the pain. I come back to earth when the doctor Stevens begin to whisper in my ear. "I'm a busy man," he say. "And I've been in this hospital for twelve hours. So make a decision, eh?" He was nervous because my first baby was a cesarean. This doctor is talking to me so no one else can hear. "When I leave this hospital, nobody's gonna be able to reach me. I don't know where I'm gonna go, I may go fishing, but I won't be answering the phone. If you get into any trouble here, you're on your own. So make a decision." Then he left the room.

Then my friend Doctor January come in. Of course, he is the anesthesiologist, if I was to have a cesarean, he will prepare me. But he is my friend and I have lost hold of this labour, I don't know how long it would take for my baby to be born in a natural way. I look at him as if to say, "What should I do?" But he cannot even meet my gaze. And I realize I am once again completely alone with a very big job ahead of me. When the nurses come in I say, "Cut me up. Do it. Do it now." But there is a problem. My friend Doctor January is unable to find the right place to put the needle in my back. He tries once. He tries again. He's shaking his head, he seems so ashamed, but this is my spine! The third time, he gets some spinal fluid in the needle, and I am beginning to get frightened. They will call another doctor, and for a long time I am waiting for this doctor. But something happens inside me when I am lying there, suddenly I am so afraid for my baby! It is a horrible feeling that wells up inside me with a blackness that is so terrifying! And I feel like I have to get this baby out right now or she will die! I get up off my back and rip the monitor off and the iv and squat down and I feel a strong rush through my body and I want to push.

A nurse tries to help. "Get your hands off me, this baby is going to give birth to itself!" My water breaks with a rush all over, black and dark and gooey, like my fear! And then everyone is freaking out. Finally I push my baby out and leave me alone like I have disappeared. But they did not bring her back to me! They are doing something over there, all of them paying frantic attention, and pumping her. Someone took me to another room, like I had no part in this at all, like there was nothing I could do for my own baby! For two hours I wait in that room! Was my baby alive? There was another woman in the bed next to me, and while I was there, they pulled the curtain around her bed. "What did she look like?" this woman ask the doctor "What colour were her eyes? How many fingers did she have?" And all he can say is, "I am sorry, sometimes babies die." I was holding this woman's hand and looking into her eyes like I was pulling her out of a sinking whirlpool, and the fear was like a monster over my head, ready to scream. So I go to look for my baby. And I did not leave her side. So you can see, I understand the question. I am the mother of these children in my womb. It is my only desperation that they should live.

The Sister Upstairs

Robert Vivian

Scene: a bedroom

Dramatic
Aunt Boat: (42) a large woman who resembles a peasant in one of Jules Breton's nineteenth century pastoral paintings

> *Aunt Boat has just poisoned her sister, House, who was too obese to leave her bed. Here, Boat addresses herself to her sister's enormous body.*

BOAT: I never minded being heavy. Even now, I'd take the weight of the world on my shoulders. Aunt House, Aunt Boat—they were always nicknames for someone else. They don't know who we are. *(Silence.)* I remember running back to the shed, breathing hard and sweaty, and closing the door behind us. Nothing moved and it smelled like gasoline. We lifted our dresses. We checked out our private parts. We wanted to know where we came from. We wanted to know why we were just a shade different than other girls our age. It had nothing to do with sex. You called me Turtle. Because my stomach was hard and round. Even then I was big for my age. There in that shed with those grimy yellow windows, I think I loved you more than any person I've ever known. Because we were sisters. We shared something. We were almost the same size. And we were healthy and sunburnt in the summer and full of happiness and the joy of running around. We had nothing to worry about. We went swimming and ate our sandwiches under a tree. *(Silence.)* House, are you listening to me? We were happy girls. If we knew how everything would turn out, would we let the other grow up? Or would we have ended it in the shed? I think you know the answer to that, honey. I think that's what we'll always have in common.

Soda Fountain

Richard Lay

Scene: a small American town. Summer, 1969

Serio-Comic
Sally: (20s) an alcoholic

> *When her fiancé shipped-off for Vietnam, Sally eventually
> turned to booze to dull her fear and boredom. Here, she
> does her best to explain why she drinks.*

SALLY: *(To herself.)* I won't talk to you ma. Oh yes, I'm here. I'm as
here as I'm gonna be. You won't hear me because people who
drink tread softly through the night, carefully putting one foot
before the other in dread of falling over or worse, losing the bottle in the dark…I don't think Johnny knows or cares. Danny
knows and I know he cares. If I was a man who drank I would
wear it like a medal on my chest. I DRINK, I could shout…but I
am a woman who drinks and that is different…a lot different. I
don't sleep with men when I drink, except friends who know the
rules and sleep with their clothes on…shoes off…That arrange-
ment is good and in the morning after surviving rival snores I turn
on 'Good Morning America' and buy some French bread and
wine and prove with polite conversation that we were just friends
and not really sleeping partners…people who sleep with their
clothes on don't even share dreams is what I say to them as I put
them in cabs while they figure out their excuses. Why do I drink?
Well I guess I like it…I guess I want the buzz that lovely buzz that
tells you that you are away with the fairies and that everything is
possible. The Soda Fountain crowd drink gallons of my vile coffee
and the only buzz they ever get is a blood pressure rush when
they get their mail and read letters from people they owe money
to…That really is a shame…So I drink until my brain is altered…I
go from boring to bright to extremely intelligent and then

extremely, extremely intelligent…Then I become a philosopher and I talk to men I would never normally glance at. They look at me from their perch at the bar and undress me in their raddled suburban brains. Forgetting to eat is a neat trick…Forgetting to live is even neater. Forgetting to drink is a mortal sin. Hail Marys all round, and make them Bloody. And one for you my imaginary bartender…What's your name, by the way?

Soda Fountain

Richard Lay

Scene: a small American town. Summer, 1969

Dramatic
Ma: (40–50) a woman grieving over the death of her son

> *When Francis is found drowned, Ma does her best to cope
> with the loss. Here, she describes how she had come to love
> this child who was born less-than-perfect.*

MA: *(Looking into distance.)* When Francis was three I wanted to
kill him because I knew he was…you know, a dime or two short.
I thought I couldn't love an idiot. And I proved myself so
wrong…he gave me strength as he struggled through all his
humiliations at school. They spat at him, threw rocks at him, said
terrible things. But through all of it he remained a constant,
cheerful kid. He knew more about affection than anybody I
know. He had an instinct about it. He knew that if I was worried
all he had to do was put his arms around me and kiss me. He
knew that if I cried—all he had to do was smile. The warmth of
our bodies meant everything. His father tried to pretend his son
didn't exist in the later years. Jim thought that somehow he had
failed.

> [PORTERHOUSE: Jim was a good man. He loved Francis in his
> own way. He never could show his emotions.]

MA: The worst thing about death is visiting graves…a mound of
earth, flowers real or plastic and the thought that the person you
love is six feet down and rotting. It's difficult to comprehend that
the person you loved so much will be a skeleton. It's difficult to
love a dead person…but Sam, I guess we want everybody to love
us when we die.

Some-Bodies

Gail Noppe-Brandon

Scene: a low-heat steam room in a NYC health club

Dramatic
Bethany: (40) an attractive, neurotic woman who has had exten-
sive face and body work to maintain the illusion

> *When Bethany encounters a long-lost childhood friend in a*
> *steam room, she finds that she must account for the unusual*
> *amount of work that has gone into creating and maintaining*
> *her "perfect" body.*

BETHANY: *(Pause.)* It s not really about change Dora, it's about *not*
changing. It's about trying to stay the same. It's about getting a
lot of attention for your little girl blonde hair, and then one day
your father comments that it's getting darker. And he says it sadly,
like he's pining for a lost friend. So you start sneaking in to the
medicine chest, and using hydrogen peroxide to get it light again.
And then you graduate to Sun-In; and then Nice N' Easy. And
then, when you're older and you have more money, you pay a
professional to do it. So it looks really natural—like it did when
you were eight. And then one day it helps to cover the gray too.
And then you dare to snip it off, those long little-girl locks. And
you think you're making a grand statement about your indepen-
dence; your refusal to be a doll. And your father, and later your
husband, say that no matter what, they'll always think of you
with your long beautiful hair. So you let it grow back, because it's
the best of you. And even though it's always getting in the way
when you work, and it takes forever to care for it, you never
make the mistake of cutting it off again. And you figure out ways
to keep your skin as smooth as a little girl's. You go through the
weekly torture of electrolysis, and waxing—which hurts like hell
and costs a lot of money. And you don't have babies so you can

keep your breasts small and your hips lean and girlish. And you smooth out your crows feet— *(Anticipating Dora's question.)* When I was thirty-five. And you live in dread fear that even though you have the face and the body of a *girl,* you're not fooling anyone. It's not good enough. Not perfect enough. *(Closing her eyes.)* You can't imagine how much I want to feel good about being a grown woman. I've never felt good about it. Because all the men are looking at eighteen year olds.

Something Blue

Michaela Murphy

Scene: here and now

Serio-Comic
Michaela: (30s) a woman attending her younger sister's wedding

Here, Michaela remembers an incident from her childhood that would become an enduring bone of contention between her and little sister Erin.

MICHAELA: I'm twelve and Erin's ten and there's a little Miss Rhode Island pageant at the carnival at Saints John and Paul church. Mom and Dad enter Erin and for the preliminaries Erin gets new clothes and a makeover at Jordan Marsh. That night as Erin twirls her baton to David Cassidy's "I think I love you" the judges fall in love and Erin is named one of five finalists competing for the Rhinestone tiara and the one-hundred dollar gift certificate at the mall. (And she's gonna win she's way prettier.). On the big day we get to the carnival really early and I beg to go on the rides. It's a small carnival so after the ferris wheel and the merry-go-round all that's left is The Moonwalk. It's this huge house-size pillow that you go inside and you jump around like a maniac. Erin takes off her brand new first pair of high heel shoes and I my sneakers and we go inside and we're having a blast. Michaela: Hey Erin check it out, you can do flips. Hey, watch me Daddy watch me. I jump high into the air and I do a perfect two and a half and I come down and I land—right on Erin's head. One half hour before the Coronation of Little Miss Rhode Island. Erin walks out of the Moonwalk with the biggest blackest eye you've ever seen. Unbearably no one says one word to me. But Dad's making all these jokes—"Hey Erin, that's my girl she'd rather fight than switch." Mom pulls out her Jackie O sunglasses and Erin gets to wear them as she struts her stuff in front of the judges. I think it

89

was when Erin stood there in front of the whole panel and went Peek-a-boo that clinched it—she lost. Erin's black eye took weeks and weeks to heal. But, hey, you should have seen the other guy.

Stars

Romulus Linney

Scene: Manhattan; a penthouse terrace on a summer night

Serio-Comic
She: (30s) a party guest making not so idle chat

> *Here, a woman describes an act of marital infidelity that she
> recently committed to a man she has just met at a party.*

SHE: So there I was. Five o'clock Saturday afternoon, Hamptons,
smiling and bored. Norwood Struther wore a blue linen blazer, a
red and yellow tie, silly and snappy. He didn't say a word. Men
liked him, slapped him on the back, called him Squeaky, kidded
him about being a bachelor, fondly, but with some kind of something else about it, I couldn't tell what. Well, I was so sick and
frustrated with my husband, mad at the world and my utterly asi-
nine position that summer in the Hamptons, hello, there,
Norwood, you squeaky bachelor, how are you, say something,
and he did. He did have this stutter and high weird voice. I was
desperate. I said, "Norwood, take me home?" He said, "Yes."
"Bartender, tell my husband I've gone to the movies." I was in
Squeaky's bedroom in half an hour. He lived right on the beach,
million dollar real estate Bridgehampton. Bedroom whole side
wall open to the sea. God. God, you could hear the surf roaring
and pounding. Wonderful. Kissing, hugging. He undressed me.
Grand. But it took him a while to undress himself. It took me a
while to notice it, then to see that he was choking, face red as a
lobster, mortified, in that ravishing home, in his beautiful bed by
the sounding sea. He had a very small sexual organ. *Very small.*
    [HE: Oh.]
SHE: He tried to apologize. I kissed him and said stop, it doesn't
matter.
    [HE: Did it?]

SHE: Of course. He wouldn't talk to me afterwards. Mumbled something about reality I couldn't understand, stuck his head under a pillow, like a little boy. I had betrayed my husband—again—this time with a poor wretch lying ungenerously bestowed next to me in abject misery. Outside on the beach, we could hear the surf pounding. The sea, powerful and potent, alive with cruelty and beauty. All that creation, and us. There was even moonlight, gorgeous, ravishing, with me and Norwood in his bed. And my husband, who hoped I liked the movie.

Sticky and Shary

Rob Handel

Scene: NYC

Dramatic
Shary: (16–18) a ghost

> *Shary committed suicide when she could no longer bare
> being secretly pregnant, her parents' violent arguments and
> being accepted at Vassar all at the same time. Here, her rest-
> less spirit recalls one of her parents' more unpleasant con-
> frontations.*

SHARY: Dad hadn't been around for a long time, and then one
night there were a couple of calls. Mom was getting upset, and
then angry. The last time it rang she just slammed it down. We
watched TV and let it do all the talking. Then the buzzer started
going and everyone jumped. Somebody insistent and we didn't
think it was the neighborhood kids. Mom yelled at him through
the intercom to just go home and he yelled stuff back. It stopped
buzzing, but I guess someone let him in 'cause a minute later he
was at the door, banging and yelling he wanted to see us. We ran
to our rooms and left Mom to deal with it. They were calling us
names of objects. I couldn't not listen, not that I had the energy
to want not to hear. I was deep into sullen charcoal eye level by
that time. By the time he did go away Mom was on the floor crying. The sign on her body said love is stupid betrayal. Sticky's
grouch mask had fallen off in the struggle. Little boys get real
confused when Mom's not strong. He looked like he wanted me
to tell him what he was supposed to do. I hugged him. Figured it
was substitute time. I felt like a babysitter. I hated babysitting and
I was the worst. He was trying to look strong anyway. Sticky never
cried. His windshield was unbreakable. I stared at the mouse hole
in the corner of my room by the desk leg. We probably didn't

have mice anymore but the hole was still there. I kept staring at it through Sticky's hair. Greasy. Probably depositing oil into the pores on my nose. I guess we got up eventually and pretended to try to sleep.

Sticky and Shary

Rob Handel

Scene: NYC

Dramatic
Shary: (16–18) a ghost

> *Shary here describes her suicide, which unfortunately claimed the life of her younger brother, Sticky.*

SHARY: The bass player from Sonic Youth appeared to me. There was this cloud of red around her like the spray hissing out of my veins changing the color of the tile, like desert sand in a psychedelic poster. "What the fuck," she said. What do you mean, Kim? Tell me what to do. "What the fuck," she said again. I was so angry at her for being there in my bathroom mirror when I was trying to kill myself, I screamed at her, WHAT? WHAT? "What the fuck, girl," she looked down her nose like I was the world's biggest fool, like I was making her sick, like I was so boring. I held up my arms and yelled at her LOOK! I'M DOING SOMETHING! ALRIGHT? WHAT DO YOU WANT FROM ME? And she *sneered* and started to turn away and I'm like, DON'T YOU CARE? WHERE DO YOU THINK YOU'RE GOING, BITCH? I'M DYING HERE! I'M BLEEDING ALL OVER MY FUCKING SELF AND YOU'RE NOT EVEN *IMPRESSED??!!* I fell down dizzy and couldn't see her in the mirror and I screamed FUCK! as I felt the delayed pain of the razor blade going into my knee. And I realized I was crying for the first time in years and years, my shirt was soaked with salt water and I saw myself sitting in this mess and I just sobbed FUCK I AM SUCH A LOSER…

But I was still there, I couldn't move but I could see the room and I wondered if I'd really shouted and would they come find me. I saw my wrists had stopped bleeding and I could only think that is just so pathetic. Immediately I wished I hadn't focused because the shock wore off my knee again and this white flashing like TV static started going on and off in my brain preventing me from putting a thought together. This rush came in and I focused on Sticky in the doorway, I was so glad to see him and not Mom but he was in slow motion, his mouth was open and I saw over the course of minutes all the color leave his face and he turned black and white and I panicked for an instant, oh no he's a hallucination, but then another channel changed and he was trying to speak and I was saying over and over, trying to be very clear, Sticky Hand Me The Towel, and his body started trying to move by itself and he tuned in enough to reach for the rack and a sound started to come out of him just as he took a step forward and pulled down the towel. It fell on my head and I heard the sound change to this squeaky howl and WHUMP his head landed in my bloody lap and I saw the blood on a new part of the floor where he'd stepped right on the other razor blade and fainted like he wanted to anyway. I was so depressed I just sighed into his poor face and I saw the first sound had come with a tear that was running down past his mouth now and with the new angle was coursing out towards his ear. I wrapped the towel around his foot, took off my shirt and bit it while I pulled the blade out of my knee, sat there breathing deeply for a while, tore the shirt and wrapped my knee up, sat on the edge of the tub and splashed cold water on myself, put on my favorite clothes and found two yellow wristbands from the summer we took tennis lessons, rifled everyone's drawers for money and tokens, found my winter coat and went to the door. I felt chilly but kind of powerful, so I could stop for a burst of sentiment: went back and threw my Sonic Youth tapes in a bag with some other stuff I thought I'd need and food from the kitchen. I was going to check on Sticky again but I didn't want to be tempted to wake him up so I took the elevator down, walked two blocks south to a pay phone and called Mrs. Gutman on the sixth floor who has a key and told her to come up right away and let herself in, Sticky was hurt. I hung up and walked down into the subway for the Port Authority.

Svetlana's New Flame

Olga Humphrey

Scene: Coney Island

Serio-Comic
Svetlana: (20s) a recent Russian émigré

> *Svetlana is starting a new life in Brighton Beach where she is*
> *beginning her American adventure by learning how to be a*
> *fire-eater for a sideshow Here, the spirited young woman*
> *muses on the etiquette of fire-eating.*

SVETLANA: How do you eat fire? What is the etiquette of swallow-
ing flames? Is it proper to hold the fire utensil in your left hand or
your right? Do you dab your lips with a napkin afterwards? What
if you get a spark caught in-between your teeth? Is it correct to
take out a small mirror to pick it out, or is it preferred that you go
to the bathroom and handle it in private? Is it gauche to give
someone a taste of your fire, or must you offer everyone their
own torch? No one ever told me the rules of proper fire-eating,
so I made up my own. First, wear red. Go all the way. If you eat
fire, be fiery. Red lipstick. A siren's dress. And very high heels.
Who cares about safety? After all, you're eating fire! You don't
play it safe to begin with. You're someone on the edge, so teeter
there all the time. "Teeter"—that's the new word I learned today.
So, this is my life as a fire-eating American. Guess what? My new
vocation consumes me in every way. But finding my calling doesn't
mean that everything is going well right now. Because it's not.

Tea Time

Dori Appel

Scene: a homeless woman's makeshift campsite

Serio-Comic
Eve: (40s–50s) a homeless woman; brash, spunky and possibly crazy

> *Here, loquacious Eve entertains passengers from a tour bus with a tale of alien visitation.*

EVE: Well, look who's here—Goggling Gray Line City Tours coming to view the homeless! Eve's got guests! *(She directs the bus.)* Come on, come on, you got room. That's it, come on, come on, come on—Whoa! *(She watches the tourists getting off the bus.)* Heyyy—we got a crowd today! Welcome, ladies and gents, step right up. *(She counts them as they alight.)* Twenty-seven, twenty-eight, twenty-nine…You love me! You're my fans! You've come for tea! Got your Brownie cameras? Got your Kodak color film? Got your Polaroids? *(She takes another jar from one of her bags and offers it to the crowd.)* Won't you come into my parlour, so to speak? I'm glad to say I can still offer matching cups. *(She addresses one of the tourists.)* Oh, the camcorder! Now that's what I call class. Up front and personal, take you right into the subject's kitchen—except in this case, *that's* the whole point. *(She does a little shimmy.)* I haven't got a *pot* to piss in, much less *kitchen* or a *house!* Oh yeah, everybody's interested in the homeless now, we're always in the news. People want to know where we sleep, how we eat, where we come from. Well, let's start with the basics, let's introduce ourselves. *(She pauses, puts one hand up to her ear and makes a beckoning gesture with the other.)* Louder, I can't hear you. *(She listens again, then says in a singsong.)* I'll tell you if you'll tell me. *(Beat.)* Okay, let me guess. *(She points.)* Curley, right? *(She points again.)* And Larry. *(She points again.)* And Moe! *(She laughs.)* Well, it's okay if you don't want to tell me. After all. *I* am the star of this show! *(She strikes a pose and smiles.)* You can call me Eve. Just don't call me Eve-il, though some have. Oh, I have to hand it to you, folks, you came to the right place. I *am* the original homeless—pitched out, exiled, deposed. Some landlord I had, a rule-stickler like you wouldn't believe. Break one clause in his fancy lease, and out you go. Forget all you did to make the place homey, forget your security deposit, forget everything! O-u-t with no notice, and that's that. *(To someone in the crowd.)* What was that, honey? No, I didn't take it before a rental board. We didn't have things like that back then. You have to understand, I've been homeless a long time. *(She listens.)* I don't know—five thousand years? Ten? Twenty? Something like that. *(Abruptly changing tone.)* Hey, anybody ready for tea? *(She raises her glass.)* No? But it's my own special blend. Moonlight Magic I call it because that's the way I brew it. Twenty-eight nights and totally delicious! *(She scans the crowd.)* Hey, how about a little reciprocity here? You all know where *I* live—so what about you? *(She listens.)* Rugby, Ohio, is that a fact? *(She listens.)* All of you? All of you are here together from the Central Rugby Interdenominational United Christian Summer Bible Class? Oh, I see! You got your bibles with you! Then you know all about it, don't you? The building of the property. The terms of the lease. The eviction of the bad, sexy broad and her luckless mate. *(Beat.)* At least you think you do. *(Changing tone.)* Rugby, Ohio, huh? Probably a real pretty place. I bet you all have your nice houses and your shiny kitchen appliances and your sliding glass doors to your patios. Oh, don't get me wrong, I don't blame you a *bit* for being curious. Everybody is. We've got tourists coming here from every place you can think of. Why, just last week there was a group of seventeen tiny Venutians pulled right up to say howdy-do, so they could tell the folks back home. *(She listens.)* No, honey, not Ven-ice. Veee-nus. And hey, they never heard those bible stories you know by heart—wouldn't recognize Genesis if it had four wheels and pig-tails, and that's the truth. But they were cute as a button and friendly as you could ever wish for. We were having tea and a cozy chat—*they* loved my Moonlight Magic—when all of a sudden along comes St. John the Baptist.—That's what we call him, lives underneath that bridge over there. And St. John, he's carrying a big bible, just like you've got, and he stops right here and begins at the beginning with The Creation of the World—which leads right up to my eviction, right? How God made this thing and saw it was good, and that thing and saw it was good, how he made my dear husband, and then made me out of his rib as a little afterthought. And you know what? Those Venutians laughed so hard the tea ran out their noses! "Tell it again!" They shouted. *(As a Venutian, laughing.)* "Tell us how— *(She laughs.)* how the man god— *(She laughs.)* how he— *(She laughs.)* how he—gave birth from his little ding-dong!" *(As herself.)* See, they thought he meant to be funny! They thought a male god giving birth to the world was a riot! But St. John, he's so mad his eyes are all aglitter, even though they keep smiling and laughing and hollering for more. "Heathens!" he shouts. "Heretics!" He's holding his bible up above his head and shaking his staff at them and—

(She stops abruptly as the tourists begin to file back to the bus.)

EVE: Hey, where you going? Don't get back on the bus now, I'm right in the middle of my story! *(Beat.)* What do you mean, "Sorry, Sadie, we're late for the next stop"? For your information, fella, Eve's the name, truth's the game, and this is the most important stop you're gonna make!

(The bus is moving away, and she runs and shouts after it.)

EVE: Listen to me! Those little Venutians had great big heads to hold their enormous genius brains, and you want to know what they said? Listen! It's important.

(The bus has pulled away. Eve stops, waves goodbye, then slowly returns to her crate, sits, and pours herself some tea.)

EVE: Every one of those super-advanced, high-tech space travelers shook my hand before they left, and the very smallest, wisest one, who I guessed was even older than I am, looked me straight in the eye and said, "Of all that is sacred, most sacred is The

Mother." And then they all just got on their funny looking bus and off they went. *(She follows the progress of the Venutian bus into the sky, then stands, holding her tea jar.)* Thanks, fellas—that was a good reminder—gave me a new lease, so to speak. *(Beat.)* Yeah, it's me. Eve. EEEEVE!

(If technically possible, the name should echo and reverberate throughout the theater. Eve listens as her name echoes to the sky, then raises her jar in a toast.)

EVE: Hey pals. here's lookin' at you!

To Each His Own
(Dead and Gone to Granny's)

Jussi Wahlgren

Scene: the garage of a family house in suburban Finland

Dramatic
Linda: (34) a woman nearly trapped in a generational cycle of subservience

> *Married to a man she doesn't love, Linda here describes her unfortunate legacy.*

LINDA: My grandmother raised my mother to serve and obey men. Well, at least her husband to be. When my father entertained his business associates, my mother served drinks and played the piano. Because my father ordered her to. He was a wholesaler in textiles. He argued with his friends about everything. Randolph Turpin vs "Sugar" Ray Robinson, Ho Chi-Minh and Vietnam, Cuba, the Kennedys and finally the Hippie movement, free love and drugs. He died listening to Elvis's Jailhouse Rock, preaching about how it demoralized the children of the revolution. I was six and I never knew which revolution he was referring to...Mother never complained, she never argued. She just did it because he wanted her to. I was the only child. My mother decided to raise me to listen to myself first. Isn't that clever? I mean she abased herself to be able to raise me differently. It's a beautiful thought anyway.

Twockers, Knockers and Elsie Smith

Jean Stevens

Scene: the kitchen of a very ordinary house

Serio-Comic
Elsie Smith: (60s) a woman planning an elaborate suicide

> *Recently, things have happened to Elsie which have convinced her that it's time to shuffle off this mortal coil. Here, the sassy granny describes the unfortunate incident which has inspired her to take her own life.*

ELSIE: Now, Senokot. When exactly should you take it? *(She looks at the writing on the tube.)* I expect the normal dose takes a few hours to work. So, if I take a couple of dozen tablets now they should do the trick. *(She starts to swallow Senokot tablets—using water or cold tea to wash them down.)* Oh, don't worry. This is a once-only job. I won't be making a habit of it. I'm not bulimic, thank God. There's not a lot to be grateful for in old age but at least you've done with all that trying to follow fashion. Couldn't keep up if I wanted to—what a pillock I'd make done up in a boob tube and a two-inch skirt. There! I enjoyed that—I don't think. If I have to make a quick exit to the lav at some point, don't be surprised. Well, as quick an exit as I can manage. *(She indicates her walking stick.)* I would like you to know that I don't normally need this. I'm pretty nifty on my pins usually but a couple of weeks ago I had a slight…altercation with a souped-up Escort. A near do, you might say. A very near do. *(She starts tidying up in the kitchen.)* I'd been to my evening class. Literature. I only went at first because our Becky persuaded me. Becky. My granddaughter. I'm ever so proud of her. She's just started at University. She said it'd give me something to do while she's away. I said, I've got plenty to do, thank you very much. Then I got to thinking, I'd better be able to hold my end up when she comes home with all her latest thoughts and theories. I'm glad I did. I've been learning bucketsful of stuff. Just let her mention alliteration or ono-matopoeia…

We're doing 'Antony and Cleopatra' at the moment. A rol-licking good story, that one. I'll be sorry not to be going any more. Glad I've been doing it, though. Nearly didn't. I thought, Literature? A lot of posh words and bugger-all action. But it's not really about words. It's about people. Our Becky knows more about words than me but she doesn't know more about people. I'm a bit ahead of her on that score. She hasn't been getting the better of me. Not that's she trying to. She's a good lass. I've been lucky really. She's dead clever and she's worked hard. Not that she hasn't been trouble, in her time. She's had me tearing my hair out on many a fraught occasion and once I didn't sleep for five weeks 'cos I didn't know what she was up to. But she's come good. She's all right. Well, really, she's more than all right, that girl. Matt, too. In his own way. He's a bit younger than Becky. He's always been a right bloody handful. Never took a blind bit of notice of me. He's always gone his own way. The word 'indepen-dent' was invented for that lad. Then he surprised me by sud-denly saying he was going to get down to some school work. I didn't think he even knew what schoolwork was. He said he was going to stay behind and do some extra, then he'd be along at his mate's house sorting out the homework. But, and there's a big but…Hang on a minute, I'd better tell you one thing at a time, and in the right order. Where was I? *(She indicates the walking stick.)* I was telling you about this, wasn't I. Well, I was coming home from my evening class one Wednesday. The 'bus didn't come—surprise, surprise—so I set off walking. My head was full of Cleopatra. We'd been reading that bit where she's screwing up her courage to do what she calls her 'noble act.' "Show me, my women, like a queen: / Go fetch my best attires…" It was all there in my mind's eye. The fertile lands of the Nile, the glories of the Egyptian palace, and the bloody awful fix she's in. Her beloved Antony dead, Caesar preparing to humiliate her, every-thing she owns, every last camel, about to be taken away. Not that she's the nicest person I've ever met. Well—met, in a manner of speaking.

She can be a right bitch, cruel too when she puts her mind to it. But not a wimp. She can go for it when she needs to. She stands up to her full height, she looks fate right in the eyes, she gives her last command to her faithful servants: "Go fetch my best attires."

So I'm not seeing what I'm walking through: the arse-hole end of Manchester—burned-out, boarded-up and buggered. I'm seeing golden figures bright in the burning sun, immeasurable marble columns, silver platters with piles of luscious fruit spilling from them, red wine cascading from jeweled pitchers into golden goblets. Never mind the dog shit on the pavement, I'm Cleopatra walking down long, shining corridors, sweeping into vast assembly rooms, rich with heavy scarlet tapestries and glowing with a cornucopia of priceless paintings and exotic carvings. Suddenly, there's a horrible screeching sound, a smell of burning, and a big red monster hurtling towards me. Then everything went into slow motion—like some hideous action replay. My hands fly out, I'm trapped by a wall, this red demon seems to grin as it comes towards me. I have to do something, so I jump to one side like a demented rabbit, then there's a final explosive crack like the whole world is shattering into bits…then nothing. I woke up in a hospital bed with people saying daft things to me, like "Oh, my dear, you were so lucky." "You can't know how lucky you've been." Well, if that's good luck, I thought, let's hope I don't get any bad luck. Turned out I'd been hit by a twocker. Well, I'd been hit by a *car* but with a twocker driving it. They started to try and explain it to me, as if I needed an explanation. Taking Without the Owner's Consent…yeah, yeah, yeah. Anyway, I ought to be thankful, I'd been *so* lucky. Then in strolls Matt. All pimples and bovver boots. "Are yer all right, Gran?" I look up. He's as white as my hospital sheets. That's a simile, by the way. And—my God he's holding out a bunch of grapes. They're a bit tacky. Look as if a locust has had first go at them. All the same, a bunch of grapes. Something not quite right here. I put my hand out for them, thank you Matt. And all the time my mind's darting hither and yon, suddenly remembering looks, remembering words, and adding two and two together till they make a hundred and two. Shit! So, it's my fault. One way or another, it really is my fault.

Vegetable Love

Tammy Ryan

Scene: Queens, NY

Dramatic
April: (30s) an alcoholic mourning the death of her father

> *Following her father's funeral, April and her sisters gather around the dining room table and catch up with one another. April is fascinated that her younger sister, Moira, is pregnant. Here, she waxes rhapsodically on the subject of creation.*

APRIL: You know what scares me? Not human catastrophes like relationships and nuclear war—we can avoid those if we're smart—we probably aren't, but if we were—we have some measure of control over those decisions—some human's finger is on the button, and it's up to him *or her*—it's up to *us* in a larger sense—to decide if we are fucking stupid or not. And that's pretty frightening too, actually, now that I'm talking about it—but not in the everyday sense. I'm able to live on some level of denial about *that.* But what punctures through the everyday veil of denial—what really really scares me in waking moments and in sleep—including a really good drunk—like now—is *Mother Nature.* There's no way to protect yourself from a really big earthquake—or an out of control tornado, a hurricane—or a—a ty*phoon.* I mean, there's no reckoning with that kind of power. Struck by light*ning?* It can happen at any time. And if we venture out further—like imagine Outer Space: *Billions* of meteors cruising like ballistic missiles, missing us by *inches?* How do we know? You know what wiped out the dinosaurs? A *rock.* A big one. It's insane. We can be wiped out by the mindless whim of Mommy Nature skipping stones across the galaxy. She smiles at us from out of Hallmark Cards, but Mommy gives away how terrifying she can be with every move she makes. *(To Moira.)* I mean, do you realize what kind of *force* has been unleashed in you? To set life in *motion?*

[MOIRA: You mean sex?]

APRIL: No, not just *sex,*—two men can have sex, two women can have sex, but they'll never unleash that *force* needed to start life. ZAP! Like lightning striking. Do you know there's only fifteen minutes in a month when a woman can get pregnant? And really when you get down to it, it's about the battle between one tiny microscopic egg and one teeny weeney tad pole sperm—*Whale.* Now where did that come from? They named a whale, the biggest creature known on the planet—after a tiny microscopic— makes you wonder. Anyway, it all comes down to a difference between one moment, really, and another, for *every person that's alive.* It's a miracle. That kind of power is impressive—and absolutely horrifying.

Vegetable Love

Tammy Ryan

Scene: Queens, NY

Dramatic
Brigit: (50s) a new widow

> *On the day of her husband's funeral, Brigit finds herself sur-*
> *rounded by her daughters. One is pregnant, one anorexic*
> *and one an alcoholic. Here, she recalls a dream she once had.*

BRIGIT: You're not supposed to dream when they give you anesthesia.

[APRIL: Shut up everybody. Mommy's talking:]

BRIGIT: When they give you anesthesia, you're not supposed to dream; you're supposed to go into a dreamless sleep; "Twilight" they called it. Only, I dreamed every time, with each of you girls, including the stillborn. The same exact dream. It didn't matter who was born yet, all of my children were in the dream, and they were all about the same age between two and three. And in the dream, I'm pulling them in this little red wagon, and I'm running away from these men in the city who want to give them this medicine that would keep them babies forever. At first, I thought it might a good idea. They wouldn't have to grow up and suffer disappointment. They could stay with me always and we'd play blocks and have tea parties and I wouldn't have to worry about teaching them things I didn't know. There'd be no problems going from stage to stage, because they'd never develop, they'd never get any older, and they'd never stop loving me—so I say yes, give them the medicine. And just when they were about to give it to them, I think, wait—maybe this isn't a good idea. There'd be stuff they'd miss if they never grew up, and who was I to decide? So, I quick put them all back into the wagon and start running out of the city when I realize, I'm missing one.

Voices in the Dark

Heidi Decker

Scene: NYC

Serio-Comic
Jane: (20s) an intense street person

> *Jane plays complicated rhythms on plastic tubs with drumsticks as she offers a passionate stream-of-consciousness diatribe on the nature of the city.*

> *(Jane sits with several plastic tubs around her, turned upside down. She has a dish set out in front filled with some change and a few dollar bills. She holds drumsticks, and as the lights fade up, she is drumming a fairly complicated beat on the items around her. She'll intermittently play while she talks…we catch her in mid conversation…mostly with herself.)*

JANE: All I'm sayin' is this, know wha'msayin'? Everybody here just minds they business. It ain't like they're bad people…it ain't like that. They just bein' polite, you know. People are into weird shit 'round here you know, and come a time when you think some shit's goin' on an' you oughta get involved like some hero or somethin'…people jump on YOUR ass for interfering in their shit. So it ain't like people ain't nice…like they don't care…they jus' mind their business. People who live outside don' understand…they're *afraid* of the city…tell stories bout *It,* wringin' their hands and noddin' at each other an' pointin' at the news an' puttin' extra locks on their cars an' scarin' the shit outa they kids…acting like you just set foot in the city some bad shit gonna happen to you. Well shit! You see some of these people…walkin' round wi' fifteen bags from fuckin' Planet Hollywood Worthless Shit Gift Shop and shit from the You're a Dumbass for Spendin' Your Money Here Disney store…flashin' wads of cash they *carry around in fuckin' bank envelopes!* Stoppin' people like ME wantin' to know can they get their picture taken with me 'cause I look like local color! Local color. Yeah, that's some funny shit. You look at me like I'm lyin' but it's the God's honest truth. Look, this is it. This is the spot. This is the middle of everything. If you can't take the heat, get the fuck out of the city.

They get all wide eyed and wonder why people on the street ain't so friendly. Like just cause I'm here, I ain't nobody...Like I ain't a person, just part of the whole city experience. Fuck that, I busted my ass to get *here*. This is a prime fuckin' location. Tourist central. Lookin' for they big adventure in the big bad city. Throwin' their money all over the place. They wonder why people wanna knock them down and take their shit away from 'em. Why? Because money is power and there's too many fuckin' stupid ass people with money already. It's just a drop in the bucket...but every little bit helps. *(Laughs.)* Aw, I'm just fuckin' witcha. Just 'cause I'm on the street here don't mean I steal shit. *(At passersby.)* I'm an artist! I'M NOT GONNA STEAL YOUR SHIT. Fuckin' nobody appreciates art anymore. You live in the city awhile, you see people look out for each other here...people from *outside* don't know it but it's true. It ain't all what's on the news...you know 'cause we all stuck here. It ain't like we can all go to the fuckin' Hamptons. You live here, you ain't goin' nowhere and we all gotta make it through the day. These buildings here...big ass skyscrapers everywhere...it's like big walls round the city, keeps everything in. That's why it's so fuckin' hot here in the summer...heat can't go nowhere, just hangs there. Shit gets caught in it. You know...shit that' *goes on* here...whatever. It's like everybody here has they own sound...everybody. Even if they don't MAKE a sound they GOT a sound, just from bein' alive, know wha'msayin'? It's like...you know when you say somethin', it's released out there in the air. You know like when an echo comes back to you. Only all these buildings...shit just keeps bouncin' off of them, back an' forth till it finds it's way out. In the summer...that heat just hangin' there...it slows it down. And at night...no horns honkin' not too many people makin' noise around ya...you listen real hard you can hear it. Them. The

echoes. You hear the whole city. You hear everybody's sounds…
all different kinds…together…like music. (*Pause.*) Like music.
Why you think I play here *at night? I'm* the *beat*…I jus' close my
eyes an' play along. It's a beautiful thing. The city that never
sleeps? Mmmmm…they got that right.

(*As the lights fade down, she begins to play in earnest…and
suddenly the audience hears the sounds of her drumming,
hundreds of drums and voices and city sounds all around
them…then slowly fading down…*)

Voices in the Dark

Heidi Decker

Scene: NYC

Dramatic
Woman: (30s) a homeless person whose time on the streets has been filled with peril

> *Here, a destitute woman offers some insight into the ghastly reality of her daily life.*

> *(Woman, early thirties, seated on a bench. She is wearing nondescript clothing. She is not sloppily dressed or particularly unkempt. She looks perfectly average. She holds an empty soda can and an unlit cigarette. She speaks candidly and matter-of-factly, with occasional bravado. She does not feel sorry for herself, or overly angry. Her experiences are relayed as simple facts. Her tone is primarily conversational, as if she's passing along advice to someone who has just asked her how she survives…and does she ever sleep.)*

WOMAN: What? What the fuck are you lookin' at? Look, I don't see any 'No Loitering' sign anyplace…I can sit here if I fuckin' want to. I ain't afraid of you. Go find someone else to fuck with. *(She remains rigid for a few seconds, then slowly relaxes, as person she was addressing moves away.)* Shit. Man, you'd think they'd find somethin' better to do. Assholes. *(Back to her conversation.)* It used to be real hard…at first, y'know…stayin' awake all the time. I…I'd pinch myself, or bite my lip sometimes, if I felt like I was dozin' off. Drew blood sometimes. I'd drink a lot of coffee, too…made me jittery as hell, but at least I was awake. After a while, though, even that didn't help. I used to sneak in some places…places where they don't kick you out right away. Laundromats are good. It'd be warm in there, all those machines hummin'…Hummm ummmmmmmm ummmmmmmm ummmmmm… 'til somebody's stupid kid comes by and kicks me, or gets their moldy-ass lollipop stuck in my hair or somethin'…I do what I got to do to get by, just like everybody else. *(Laughs.)* Hell, girl's gotta eat, right?

(Trails off…then, more brightly.) It ain't all bad, y'know…*this,* I mean. Hell, I'm my own boss! That's more than you can say for most girls you see on the street. I can't really blame 'em though…they just want someone to look out for them. Y'know, someone to care. *(Laughs.)* You can get someone to take care of you…all you gotta do is fuck every guy who's got fifty bucks, give your man forty-five of it, and fuck him and his friends for free. Nobody's afraid of a woman on the street. Well…yeah, if you're drooling and talkin' to martians with shit in your pants then maybe…but just a normal woman? Nah. Hell, it's like we're free. People figure what the fuck, they ain't nobody, who's gonna give a shit? You see, here's the thing: Some people roam around, angry all the time, y'know, fightin' with…ghosts. Still hurtin' so much from shit that happened *years* ago that they see it everywhere they go. They'll see their mother's face on some stranger on the street…So they go lookin'. Lookin' for somethin' to…to make it go away… somethin' smaller than them that they can hold down with one hand, maybe. Make 'em feel strong. Sometimes it's a stray dog they find and set on fire for fun. Sometimes it's you.

(Pause.) My old man was like that…he'd look like a zombie or somethin' sometimes…like his brain, y'know the good part, the nice part, just up and left. Left his face all empty. Not even any trace of me on it. I was lucky, though…'cause when I got out here, I already knew what to look for…Look out for. You can look…look into their eyes and they're not even there. All you can see are ghost faces…mean, angry…faces. In their eyes. After a while, y'know, when you know what to look for…you can tell who they are from a distance. You can see 'em comin'. I can. You just gotta watch out for 'em. You just gotta watch… *(Pause.)* So, no, I don't sleep…much. I just…I just try to dream with my eyes open.

(She takes a final drag from the cigarette, and blows the smoke up into the air as she glances down the street. Lights fade.)

The Wax Cradle

Jo J. Adamson

Scene: the home of Bronson Alcott. Concord, Massachusetts

Dramatic
Louisa Mae Alcott: (45) a writer; an unhappy woman

> *When her mother's health deteriorates, Louisa finds herself facing the inevitable conclusion that she will soon die. Plagued by nightmares, Louisa here describes one to her father and sister.*

LOUISA: As I look around at the three of us I'm reminded of my dream last night. I'd come home to Concord after being in Europe and instead of finding Orchard House there was a great stone castle. A huge drawbridge was up and the guard at the gate made me understand that I could gain entry if I knew the right words. I am a writer of children tales, I told him. Were the right words to be found in any of my books? No, he said that my books were tales told by an idiot. Signifying nothing. Now, here was the curious thing, as he talked his face began to change. He became older, wrinkled. In my fear I began to call out words, but when they passed my lips they weren't words at all, but only sounds of grating, grinding machinery. The guard's face changed again and he became...a healthy Beth. Before I could say anything else, he'd lost his hair. And his face changed shape and he became Bethie on her death bed. I cried out but there was only the tortured sound of steel scraping steel. Bethie's face changed again...into *you,* father. I said 'it's me Father, Louy. But you didn't recognize me. You turned into mother as a young girl, then a middle-age matron, finally an invalid. She turned her eyes on me and I couldn't turn away. Her face became my face, and then I *knew.* We are the belladonna and the night shade, I said. And then the drawbridge was lowered and I walked into the castle. Inside I found only broken stones and scattered crockery. *(Louisa looks down at her hands.)* It was very strange.

Wedding Dance

Dominic A. Taylor

Scene: Chicago

Dramatic
Bessie: (20s) an African American woman trying to keep it all together

> *When Bessie is admonished for not praying regularly to God by her wheelchair-bound mother, the pragmatic younger woman takes the advice offered and offers the following prayer.*

BESSIE: OK, God. We are over here in a new spot. Mom says you are still looking out, so I'm just shouting out at you. I aint looking for nothing. I'm coming straight up hollering at you. I aint asking for nothing, not for me anyway. It aint all that deep, I mean like I think you need to check out momma. She been working on your vineyard a long time so to speak. It aint like rocket science or nothing, but I mean like, don't you think she should catch a break? Every once in a while give the woman a break. She been taking that great your reward in heaven line, and running it in the ground. It's not like I think she should get a gold watch or nothing. I'm just saying why you making her suffer so much. I mean like, can't you cut her some slack on earth. I want momma living like a big dog up in heaven, and I don't want to take any stars away, but some of this stuff is excessive. There are some miserable muth…people down here who could do with some afflicting. Momma pray all the time. She in church every Sunday, and they aint even got a ramp for her at church. She goes to visit the sick, when they never came to visit her when she was in the hospital. When we lost the apartment, she was still steady dropping in ten percent of the aid check. I have no idea what the church did when she put the food stamps into her envelope. And why she going out like this? Cause she love you God. But I mean you be sending down some hard love Big G. She gets out there and casts bread on the waters while her stomach is growling. I know you aint no spiteful god. I know that. I also know that the sins of the father get passed down…but she aint know her father; so can that make you cut her some slack. Not that I need to tell you your business, but pass the sins of the father exclusively to sons. She aint never had no beef with you about nothing. Even when you sent down that trifling father of mine. And when after all this shit, sorry, all she does is pray harder, and harder. I just look at her. I don't say nothing. I know you aint used to speaking to me, but all I'm saying is give her some joy. I know she want to dance with Tyrone. I know she want to walk again…I know a month is short notice for a miracle, SO I aint asking for that. Just bring her some joy and less pain. I know that I don't put in that time praising your name the way she does…I mean god just be looking out. Oh, and fire her guardian angel, cause he be napping. I mean just take a peep at the whole situation, and see what you come up with. Peace out. Oh yeah, Amen.

Went Down to the Crossroads

Philip Goulding

Scene: the southwest of England

Dramatic
Mantha: (20–30) a young woman whose life has been forever changed by violent crime

> *Mantha's boyfriend, Davy, went on an unexpected and unexplained killing spree. Several years later, Mantha has started a new life with a new man. The past cannot be silenced, however, and she is soon tracked down by a journalist seeking the "truth." Here, Mantha speaks about Davy to the persistent journalist.*

MANTHA: It s difficult to say really. I mean you just have to get on with your life, don't you…?

[LAURA: Sure…]

MANTHA: And sometimes…for moments like, I almost forget Davy existed. I mean…I know he still does…somewhere, but…

[LAURA: I imagine it's still difficult.]

MANTHA: It's seeing the same places everyday. Everytime I walk into that shop I half-expect to see old Daniels. They were alright, him and his missus. Oh they could be a bit old-fashioned, a bit 'off,' but we all has our off-days don't we? They hadn't been here long. Couple of years at the most. They didn't deserve that, no way. No-one does, do they?

[LAURA: You must have been very shocked by what Davy did.]

MANTHA: Course I was.

[LAURA: I mean…that he could do it.]

MANTHA: I don't think he was himself, really, do you? When he done it. I mean, he liked the old army books and that but he weren't really a violent bloke. We had our rows but nothing…you know? We were just friends really. That's the truth of it. I don't think he even fancied me that much. He didn't seem to want the normal things. Never mentioned kids or nothin. He could be a laugh mind. And we had a kiss and a cuddle and stuff. Went off on adventures and things.

[LAURA: Adventures?]

MANTHA: Just off places. Nothing special. He could be quite kind. I mean, you'd never have thought he could do what he did. Not that. *(Pause.)* I could have been one of them, you know? That's what gets me. So easily. And then I wouldn't be here to tell the tale. I almost feels guilty. Maybe it were me he meant to get. Not all them strangers.

[LAURA: I understand you were the last person to see him. Before it happened?]

MANTHA: That's right. Thing is…people ask me…sounds stupid really…'How could you let him?' You know…those hands. As if…I mean, how could I know? People don't have what they are written on their foreheads do they? Besides, people you know just don't do that kind of thing. Goes to show, don't it? What does anyone know? About anybody? I don't even really know who you are.

[LAURA: Well.]

MANTHA: I take your word for it of course. You seem genuine enough. I calls myself 'Sam' now by the way.

What Cats Know

Lisa Dillman

Scene: here and now

Dramatic
Therese: (30s) a manipulating player of games

> *When her partner hears word that a friend from his past has died, Therese reveals a bit of the spleen that has helped to make her the hard woman she has become.*

THERESE: When my father killed himself, I knew it the minute I came home and found the house empty. When my aunt finally showed up and told my brother and me what had happened, I said "I know" and went out to play with my friends. I played through dinnertime and long after dark. Then I went inside and straight to my room. I heard my aunt tell my uncle I was the chilliest child she'd ever seen. She said it'd all catch up with me at the funeral. You think I cried at the funeral?

[GREGORY: I know you didn't.]

THERESE: I didn't. I sat there on that bench with my father's relatives who'd hated him and I cursed him the whole time. I didn't curse him for checking out early. I didn't curse him for leaving a chunk of his brain in the upstairs bathroom. I cursed him for all the little things. For making me compete for *everything* at my school. For calling me beanpole and Dachau in front of my friends. For sitting on the pot behind a closed door while I peed my pants in the hall. He did. He made a tribal ritual out of taking a shit. My whole family would be holding their crotches in the hall while he sat in there with a magazine having a nice leisurely dump. *(Beat.)* I cried later. Much later. When I graduated cum laude, because it was the first thing I'd ever done that I actually felt *positive* my father would approve of. And when I realized that, I also realized that it held no meaning for me whatsoever. It was the most empty moment of my life.

When a Diva Dreams

Gary Garrison

Scene: Diva's, a cabaret in New Orleans

Serio-Comic
Marty: (20–30) a young woman seeking a career in show business

> *Marty has just been hired as the new act at Diva's, a club that usually headlines singers. Marty, whose act is more like performance art than anything else, here does her best to describe her elation at being hired to the mega-divas who perform regularly at the club.*

MARTY: Well…I've never belonged to anything, 'cause I get a little nervous in groups. No clubs, or teams, or Girl Scouts, or sororities, or study groups,—nothing. And when I've tried to force myself to be a part of a group, I just faint…but I mean, *really* faint—out cold—eyes back, drool everywhere…You don't make many friends that way. I mean, I was a novelty when I was a kid—I got invited to everyone's party just on the chance I'd faint for them and hopefully droop into the cake or punch or hamburger meat. But then my novelty wore off and I realized I was spending more time getting propped up by broom handles in a corner somewhere than actually annoying the party. I always thought that it was just me—that I didn't WANT to be a part of ANYTHING. Then about three months ago, I took a bus to New Orleans—just to get away from Shreveport—and I walked in here by accident. I stood right back there, because it was crowded and there weren't any seats. And ya'll were singing this big, group song that went something like "Friends will lift your heart up when life has let you down…"

[MISS RED: "Friends and Neighbors."]

MARTY: Right. Right! That's what it was called: "Friends and

121

Neighbors." That was it. Anyway, I barely remember the song, but I'll never forget how you all looked. Music was soft, and Miss Red was singing something so full of—love—and I looked at you… *(To Penny.)* …and this—feeling—was all over your face… *(To Crystal.)* …and you had tears in your eyes… *(To Dee-Dee.)* …and I saw you in the audience, and your face was—beaming—every word meant something to you. And when the song was over, the audience clapped and whistled and cheered for you. *(Softly.)* And you took each other's hands, and bowed…and held on to each other. You didn't let go.

[PENNY: I remember that.]

MARTY: And then you hugged each other. On stage, in front of this whole—group—of people. And everyone was smiling and cheering. And I thought, well…I thought, something happened here, and it had something to do with why people want to be with other people…and I want to know what that is…I've looked everywhere for what you have here every day of your lives. I don't know what is, or what it's called. But if I don't get it, I'm not going to make it. It's that real to me. It's that…necessity. *(Smiling.)* You know, just standing here, I feel calmer than I have in my whole life. And I don't want to move.

When a Diva Dreams

Gary Garrison

Scene: Diva's, a cabaret in New Orleans

Dramatic
Miss Red: (50s) the proprietor of Diva's, a woman with drive and moxie

> *When Miss Red is incapable of paying the mortgage, it looks as though Diva's will have to be closed. Enter Delle, Miss Red's estranged sister who has more than enough money to keep the cabaret afloat, if only Miss Red can forgive her for walking out on the family. Here, Miss Red describes the effect that Delle's running away had on their father.*

MISS RED: That you do, honey. Why, you were hardly eighteen when you stood up at the dinner table and announced with your shoulders back, head up and chin high that you didn't need your family, you didn't need your sister, you were ashamed of all of us for being so—"common," is what I think you said.

[DELLE: *(Rising anger.)* You're taking that out of context! You know damn well…]

MISS RED: What I KNOW is you left a mama and daddy heartbroken, and a sister holding a handful of dreams. You left a whole neighborhood wondering why THEY weren't good enough for you. You left a whole town of people feeling ashamed for being who they were. THAT'S WHAT I KNOW! *(Louder.)* And even though you got as far away as you could, and went to a big, old impressive college and took to studying Broadcast Journalism, what I *know* is you never once—in all that time—called your mama and daddy and brought them back into your life. But they were proud of you anyway. Daddy told anybody who would listen how proud he was of you…And he wanted to tell you, too. *(Rising anger.)* For ten years he wanted to tell you. Every day he waited for that phone to ring—that call to come. And every time that phone rang, and it wasn't you, he swore under his breath, wiped his forehead…and waited for the next call. *(Walking to her.)* He never gave up, bless his soul. He'd sit by that pitiful Magnavox t.v., those rabbit ears twisted almost in half to get a good picture of you on CNN. Yeah, honey, he'd scream from the back of the house: "There she is. There's my girl. She's in China, Mama. Our baby girl's in China!" or, "She's in Moscow, Mama. Look at our girl. Wouldn't I just love a phone call?" And he'd wait. And when your call never came, and this is the worst, he started imagining the phone would ring. We'd be sitting at the dinner table and he'd say, "Emmy Jo, get that phone." Do you know how many times I answered a goddamn phone that didn't ring? *(Closer to her.)* At the nursing home, he 'bout drove those poor people crazy, 'cause you know a phone's ringing there all the time. Everybody knew he was hangin' on just to get that call. He didn't weigh more than sixty pounds—that's what cancer does to you—and he'd be wallerin' in his own mess and still be asking for the phone. Wouldn't die. Wouldn't give up. *(Quietly.)* So I had to call him…and tell him I was you, and that it was okay to die. And he finally got to say, "I sure am proud of you, baby girl."…He was gone that night. Mama followed, a week to the day. *(Cold.)* After they passed, and I was all alone, I understood what somebody like you can do to a family. *(In her face.)* Did you ever—for just one moment—hurt? Did you ever cry about any of it? Had a sleepless night? One regret? One goddamn moment of sorrow? AND DO YOU REMEMBER THE LAST THING YOU EVER SAID TO ALL OF US WAS "I'LL NEVER FORGET YOU." AND DO YOU REALIZE YOU DID?

Whiteout

Jocelyn Beard

Scene: the home of John Creek; a white separatist and militia leader, Idaho

Dramatic

Rebecca Tattinger: (60) the wife of a powerful and well-liked African American US senator facing-off against the enemy during a blizzard

> *Dan Tattinger's private plane has crashed on land belonging to John Creek, the leader of the country's largest private militia. Onboard the plane was Tattinger's secret illegitimate daughter. Public knowledge of this woman's existence could prove lethal to his political career. Dan has gone to Creek to beg help in rescuing his daughter. Rebecca, a woman of enormous intelligence and power, arrives soon after. When Creek's daughter reveals that she already knows everything there is to know about Dan and Rebecca from their intelligence group, Rebecca angrily explains why the racists know nothing about her.*

REBECCA: I will not sit in this house. The fact that the soles of my shoes have to touch your floors is bad enough…

[HELEN: Why is that?]

REBECCA: Let me tell you something about me, Miss Creek. Let me tell you something that might help you to understand me, since that's your job. Let me tell you about my Great-grandmother. My Great-grandmother was a slave, Miss Creek. Her name was Effie.

[HELEN: Oh.]

REBECCA: Don't you "oh" me, you…you…Peckerwood piece of white trash!

[HELEN: Oh, come on, Mrs. T. Everyone in the world knows

that you're descended from slaves. That alone is fifty percent of the appeal.]

REBECCA: We are *all* descended from slaves, you ignorant girl. My great-grandmother *was* a slave. Her name was Effie. She was kept on several plantations outside of Richmond, on the James River. Seems she wasn't much of a worker, but she was smart. Smart enough to keep herself out of the fields and out of the Boss's bed. Smart enough to head north when the war was over and Negroes were free to finally get paid to be slaves. Great-grandmother Effie made her way first to Philadelphia, where she worked for several years in the household of an umbrella tycoon...can you imagine making your fortune making umbrellas? That's white luck for you. Anyway, there was smart, clever Great-grandmother Effie cooking up a storm for the umbrella tycoon in Philadelphia when, as her own personal luck would have it, one of the umbrella tycoon's houseguests fell in love with her Liquor Pudding...

[HELEN: Liquor Pudding?]

REBECCA: In the south, Miss Creek, African American cooks labored to concoct countless dishes irresistible to white men... most of them so high in fat that coronary units should be on stand-by whenever they're served. Call it a sweet revenge. Liquor pudding was Effie's specialty, and a rich politician from New York City by the name of Benjamin Morse fell in love with it. He offered Effie three times what the umbrella tycoon was paying her to come and cook for him in New York and she said, "Yes, Boss. That do sound good to me." She was quite lucky. Great-grandmother Effie grew famous in New York for her unusual culinary skills and for her beauty. In fact, Morse's youngest son, Ezekial, had ardently courted Effie since her arrival. She eventually bore him three sons and three times that in scandal. Fortunately, the younger Morse was a responsible white boy, and he set Effie up in a little house in Cold Spring, right on the Hudson River, where he continued to visit even after his marriage to a Connecticut heiress. My grandfather, Thomas Morse, grew up with his mother and brothers in that little house on the river

126

and they wanted for nothing. Thomas was able to go to college, and then had the audacity to start his own law practice in Poughkeepsie, New York, in 1922. He married the daughter of one of his first clients, a man by the name of Euclid Strange who owned an apple orchard deeded to him by a grateful former employer. My grandmother, Tabitha Strange had grown up on that apple orchard, up in the Hudson Highlands. Grandma Tabby bore Effie six beautiful grandchildren: Euclid, Thomas, Nathan, Philip, Marie and my mother, Willa. Uncle Euclid and Nathan went into law with Grandfather, as did my mother. By the time I was born, Morse, Morse and Wooley was one of the biggest firms in the valley. A black law firm. It was a freak of nature. Both my parents were attorneys. I grew up in a small town named Red Hook that was as white as white can be. *We* were as white as white can be. Our neighbors were white, our friends were white, we spoke like whites, we ate like whites, we *were* white. I went to a private girl's school with a bunch of other white girls and then on to Harvard and Harvard Law. On the day I was graduated I received a rare and unexpected summons from Cold Spring. I was to present myself to Great-grandmother Effie without delay. I'd only met her a handful of times in my life and truth be told, she had always terrified me. But I was young, fancied myself white and had a JDL from Harvard in my pocket, so I drove down to Cold Spring as requested. I'd never been to the house, nor had anyone prepared me for it. The me that you seem to think you know was last seen standing in that driveway on that hot June day.

[HELEN: *(Interested.)* What happened?]

REBECCA: From the driveway, you followed a path through thick forsythia and hydrangea trees to a clearing where Effie's house had stood since a Dutch farmer had built it in the early eighteenth century. As I stood there, staring the house...or what had become of it...I didn't think of Holland, I thought of Senegal. Effie had used the years to transform that little Dutch colonial into her memory of the hut in which her mother had been born in Senegal. She'd done it all by herself. She'd even replaced the slate roof with sweet-smelling thatch. I must tell you, Miss Creek, that it quite took my breath away. It was like a memory of a dream. I found her in a herb garden on the other side of the house. She was singing…in Senegalese, dressed in a batik robe of the brightest blues I'd ever seen. Her hair was white, and piled on her head in braids. She must have smelled me, standing there behind her, for she stopped singing and slowly turned around. Her face was ancient, but somehow, still beautiful. In fact, the most startling thing about her, I remember, was that she stood erect; as if life and all its burdens had no claim on her. As if she'd never been a slave. She eyed me up and down, and then she did something I never would have expected.

[HELEN: What?]

REBECCA: She laughed, oh good lord how she laughed! She took one look at me in my white clothes with my straightened hair and the look of white concern on my face and she just laughed. She walked with a cane that she didn't seem to need, and she poked it at me and said: "Look at you, child. All dressed up and no place to go." Well, I wasted no time informing her that I did in fact have many places to go…but she cut me off with another poke of her cane and said, "You listen to me, girl child. I got no time to be listening to no pretend white girl, so you just listen to me. By this time next year I'll be dead. My bones be crushed and ground to paste the earth. Now, I been carrying something…carrying it with me all the way from Virginia, and it's heavy, girl child. Too heavy for me to take with me to the grave. I got to give it to someone to carry to the next one…and you're the one who has to take it. You. Only you."

[HELEN: What was it?]

REBECCA: She reached inside her gown, and pulled out a long necklace. I remember her hands…like little brown spiders…running up and down the necklace as they undoubtedly had every day for seventy years. "This is what I got to give to you, girl child," she said, "but I'm going to keep it on just a little while longer while I introduce you to them."

[HELEN: Them?]

REBECCA: *(As she slowly pulls the necklace out of her own dress.)* It was long, white pearls held together by black and white strands… *(She holds up the first "pearl," which is actually a human tooth, as Effie.)* "This be Rummy. The Boss man done whipped him dead. Whipped him so bad that the blood spray all over his Nile green frock coat that little Bess done took more'n a month to sew. Rummy die screamin'. *(The next "pearl.")* This be Old Paw. The Boss Man done whipped him dead. Old Paw my father's brother. Old Paw keep me from the men on the boat over. Old Paw die screamin'. *(The next "pearl.")* This be Ben. The Boss Man done whipped him dead. Ben and me was in love. I had Ben's baby in me but the Boss Man punched it out. Ben die screamin'. *(The next "pearl.")* This be Fifi. The Boss Man done whipped her dead. Fifi was my mama. She held me close in the boat over and not even let go on the block. Fifi slap Boss Man when he take my baby. Fifi die screamin'.

[HELEN: *(Quietly.)* Please stop.]

REBECCA: These are the teeth and the hair of my family. This is all I have. This pitiful ossuary. This is all I have to prove who and what I am. I don't have someone's wedding gown, passed down through generations…I don't have corsages, carefully preserved in plastic…I don't have scrapbooks or photos…all I have are these, yanked from the skulls of my forbears…these, and a great recipe for Liquor Pudding. Great-grandmother Effie gave me a powerful gift that day in her garden, Miss Creek; she gave me the gift of a secret identity. She gave me my destiny. On that day I was made a racist, Miss Creek. Just as you have been made a racist. What you need to know…what isn't in my FBI profile, is that my racist agenda is no less savage than yours.

[Helen regards her with silent appreciation.]

REBECCA: That is why I cannot and why I will not touch a single thing in *this* particular house. Do I make myself clear?

Permissions
Acknowledgments

NOTE: These monologues are intended to be used for audition and class study; permission is not required to use the material for those purposes. However, if there is a paid performance of any of the monologues included in this book, please refer to these permissions acknowledgment pages to locate the source who can grant permission for public performance.

of mechanical or electronic reproduction, such as CD-ROM, CD-1, information storage and retrieval systems and photocopying, and the rights of translation into foreign languages, are strictly reserved. Particular emphasis is laid upon the matter of readings, permission for which must be obtained from the author's agent in writing. Contact: Berman, Boals & Flynn, 208 West 30th Street, #401, New York, NY 10001, Attn: Judy Boals, Author's Agent

Epic Poetry Copyright © 1997 by James Bosley, all rights reserved. Reprinted by permission of Rosenstone/Wender. Contact: Rosenstone/Wender, 3 East 48th Street, New York, NY 10017, (212) 832-8330, Attn: Ronald Gwiazda, Author's Agent

F.O.B. To U-Haul Copyright © 1998 by Steven Tanenbaum, all rights reserved. Reprinted by permission of the author. Contact: Steven Tanenbaum, 440 West 24th Street 14E, New York, NY 10011

Forget-Me-Not Copyright © 1998 by Richard Lay, all rights reserved. Reprinted by permission of the author. Contact: Richard Lay, 205 West 15th Street 2M, New York, NY 10011, (212) 929-3423

Four Queens—No Trump Copyright © 1998 by Ted Lange, all rights reserved. Reprinted by permission of the author. Contact: Ted Lange, 7420 Corbin Avenue # 17, Reseda, CA 91335

A Garden Of Women Copyright © 1998 by Ludmilla Bollow, all rights reserved. Reprinted by permission of the author. Contact: Ludmilla Bollow, 314 West Sugar Lane, Milwaukee, WI 53217, e-mail: bollow@earthlink.net

Golden Elliot Copyright © 1994 by Linda Stockham, all rights reserved. Reprinted by permission of the author. Contact: Linda Stockham, e-mail: lstockha@wiley.csusb.edu

Gunshy Copyright © 1998 by Richard Dresser, all rights reserved. Reprinted by permission of the author. Contact: The Joyce Ketay Agency, 1501 Broadway Suite 1908, New York, NY 10036

Hazing The Monkey Copyright © 1997 by Marcus A. Hennessy. Reprinted by permission of the author. Contact: Marcus A. Hennessy, 827 9th Street #6, Santa Monica, CA 90403

Icarus Copyright © 1997 by Edward Sanchez. Reprinted by permission of the author. CAUTION: Professionals and amateurs are hereby warned that performance of *Icarus* is subject to royalty. It is fully protected under the copyright laws of the United States of America, and of all countries covered by the International Copyright Union (including the Dominion of Canada and the rest of the British Commonwealth), and of all countries covered by the Pan American Copyright Convention and the Universal Copyright Convention, the Berne Convention and of all countries with which the United States has reciprocal copyright relations. All rights, including professional, amateur/motion picture stage rights, recitation, lecturing, public reading, radio broadcasting, television, video or sound recording, all other forms of mechanical or electronic reproduction, such as CD-ROM, CD-1, information storage and retrieval systems and photocopying, and the rights of translation into foreign languages, are strictly reserved. Particular emphasis is laid upon the matter of readings, permission for which must be obtained from the author's agent in writing. Contact: The Joyce Ketay Agency, 1501 Broadway Suite 1908, New York, NY 10036, Attn: Carl Mulert, Author's Agent

In Search Of The Red River Dog Copyright © 1997 by Sandra Perlman, all rights reserved. Reprinted by permission of the author. Contact: Sandra Perlman, PO Box 906, Kent, OH 44240

Jackie: An American Life Copyright © 1991 by Gip Hoppe, all rights reserved. Reprinted by permission of the author. Contact: For Non-First Class Rights: Samuel French, 45 West 25th Street, New York, NY 10010. All other rights: Gip Hoppe c/o Bret Adams, Ltd, 448 West 44th Street, New York, NY 10036

The Joy Luck Club Copyright © 1997 by Susan Kim, all rights reserved. Reprinted by permission of Writers & Artists Agency. Contact: Writers & Artists Agency, 19 West 44th Street Suite 1000, New York, NY 10036, Attn: Greg Wagner, Author's Agent

133

134